Also by Neale S. Godfrey

Money Doesn't Grow on Trees

Why Money Was Invented

Here's the Scoop:
Follow an Ice Cream Cone Around the World

A Penny Saved

Making Change

Neale S. Godfrey's Ultimate Kid's Money Book

A Money Adventure: Earning, Saving, Spending, Sharing

MOM, INC.

TAKING YOUR WORK SKILLS HOME

Neale S. Godfrey

with Tad Richards

Simon & Schuster

SIMON & SCHUSTER
Rockefeller Center
1230 Avenue of the Americas
New York, NY 10020

Copyright © 1999 by Neale S. Godfrey/
Children's Financial Network, Inc.
All rights reserved,
including the right of reproduction
in whole or in part in any form.

SIMON & SCHUSTER and colophon are registered trademarks
of Simon & Schuster Inc.

Designed by Meryl Sussman Levavi/Digitext, Inc.

Manufactured in the United States of America

1   3   5   7   9   10   8   6   4   2

Library of Congress Cataloging-in-Publication Data:
Godfrey, Neale S.
Mom, Inc. : taking your work skills home
Neale S. Godfrey with Tad Richards.
p.   cm.
1. Home economics.   2. Women—Time management.
I. Richards, Tad.   II. Title.
TX147.G58   1999
640—dc21   99-12861   CIP
ISBN 0-684-80793-9

Acknowledgments

Thanks to all who have helped to create *Mom, Inc.* by being supporters, moms, dads, kids, and most of all, friends.

Kyle, Rhett, Alison, Linda, Beth, Malla, Mom, Herb, Sue, Gwen, Marylou, Alice, David, Jimmy, Dr. Anna, Kathy, David, Dr. Julie, Ruth, Sandy, Rick, Drew, Jill, Mural Man, Mike Rokosi, Ron, Eric, Judy, Peter, Syd, Metal Man, Elaine, Kim, Alan, Tasha, Marlene, Dana, Maxi, Phyllis, Eric, Melba, Pat, Carol, Joel, Noah, Jordan, Cathe, Miracle Man, Esther, Gil, Whitney, Nina (Irene), Kelly, Jason, Mitch Slater, Steve, Kimberly, Debbie, Caitlin, Len, Peg, Cara, Cori, Irv, Trevor, Fern, Betsy, Tennis Steve, Dr. Bruce, Dr. Barbara, Fay, Elizabeth, LeGrande, Rasheek, Lady Suzanne, and special thanks to Miss Marjorie Arp, my first-grade teacher, who taught me how to write. Without her it would have been impossible to create this book.

My mother, Georgine Axelrod, taught herself

how to be a working mother.

Georgine taught me how to be a working mother.

This book is for her, with all the love

and respect in the world.

Contents

Part III: FAMILY FRIENDLY 197

Part I

Taking It Home

Chapter 1

Home, Office, and Stress

Imagine two women sitting across from each other at a desk. The first one is Alison. At forty-two, Alison is the vice president of a successful manufacturing company. Today she has to make a decision on major capital improvements, including deciding whether to buy $20 million worth of new machinery; she has to review the résumés of several applicants for a new plant manager's position; she has to talk to lawyers and prepare a strategy for a zoning easement that will enable the company to expand an existing plant; and she has to speak to a civic club luncheon for which she has no time, but it might make a difference when it comes to getting that easement. Right after lunch, she has to head for the airport to catch a plane to the Midwest to tour a plant that might have to be closed down.

Across the desk from her is Peg, thirty-four, her secretary. Today Peg has to type up about twenty letters, some of which she'll essentially have to compose, to various suppliers and clients. She has to make copies of Alison's internal company report, bind it, and distribute it to all the company's executives. She has to check on all the changes in Alison's scheduler and make sure they're put into the computer. She has to screen all Alison's calls and appointments, deal politely but firmly with a couple of people who've showed up without appointments, and call to double-check scheduling and reservations to make sure that there aren't any snags on Alison's trip. She also has to learn the new database system the company has decided to install.

Which one of these women is under the most stress?

The answer: they both have about the same amount of stress. It's a lot, and relatively little of it is related to the demands made on them by work. Each woman is very good at what she does and takes pride in her work. Each has consistently received favorable work evaluations, even commendations.

Where does the stress come from? Alison is a single mother of two. Her ten-year-old son, Trevor, has a soccer game for the county championship this afternoon. Her fourteen-year-old daughter, Whitney, is starting to skip school and hang out with a group of girls Alison doesn't approve of. Right now, the only thing they're doing that Alison knows about is smoking cigarettes, but it's still cause for serious concern. Alison took time off from work yesterday to talk to her daughter's guidance counselor; to make up for the lost time, she had to bring work home and stay up late into the night to finish it.

Peg's husband, Mike, works second shift, so scheduling time for discussing the kids, for sex, or even for a movie or a relaxing conversation is never easy. Vincent, their fifteen-year-old son, who has always done well in school, just brought home two C-minuses and a D on his last report card. Peg sees her dream of his acceptance into a good college jeopardized. Billy, their four-year-old, has been doing well in day care—but the center is closing down, and Peg is going to have to start searching for a new source of child care.

Both of these women know the truth that every woman knows: it's not the work that'll get you . . . it's everything else.

But we're talking about two bright, talented women here—women who know how to make very complicated things run smoothly and who take legitimate pride in doing it. Why shouldn't they be able to make their home lives run smoothly?

We'll get to know Peg and Alison better as we go along. But actually, we're talking about all of us. You, me, every woman who has ever worked for a living, who has ever gone out of the house to take on a new, complex, sometimes hostile world.

We have done it. We really have changed the world. We've remade the workplace, we've remade the image of who women are in the world. There's more to be done yet—a lot more—but look at what we've done already!

We've also exploded the myth of the superwoman, the one who can bring home the bacon and fry it up in the pan (besides, we also know about all those nitrates and fats these days).

Or have we? Maybe we're still putting that same pressure on ourselves to succeed in both worlds. Many of us have husbands who do help out more around the house and who do share the responsibility of child care, a lot more than our fathers did for our mothers. For others of us, unfortunately, that's not the case. And many of us are single parents, coping with work and home all by ourselves, with no help at all.

Some help, very little help, no help . . . but here's the bottom line. Home is still our responsibility. Ultimately, it's the one that most of wouldn't trade for anything, but still it's the one that drives us the craziest and brings out complicated and ambivalent feelings.

• • •

In this book, we'll be dealing with the problems *around* dealing with the problems of our families. I'm not going to tell you how to help a troubled teenager do better in school. I'm going to show you how we can make ourselves better equipped to deal with that and other problems.

I'll be giving you reports from the front: interviews with women who have been there, women who have taken on the job of CEO in their own homes and project manager for the projects they've created.

I've changed their names and some details of their lives, and in a couple of cases they're composites, but essentially, these are women who've made it work and who have taken the time to think about what they've done and how it's worked for them.

Mom, Inc. is a self-help book for women who have management and organizational skills that they're not fully utilizing for the biggest management job of all. It's a book about how we can bring our home lives and our work lives back into a state of synchronicity and how we can bring home some of the coping mechanisms and organizing principles we've learned, developed—or innovated—at work. I'm going to show you that this is what you know, this is what you can do, these are tools you already have, and here's a new way of using them.

There are two kinds of books on organizing your home, your life, your kids. In the first, you get doctrines propounded by fearsomely efficient Home Dictators, setting up a kind of Brady Bund of routines, rules, and doctrines guaranteed to obliterate all personalities and individual foibles, and create a gleaming, sanitized paradise. There aren't a bunch of laughs in these books—there's no time for them, unless they're scheduled in. In the second, the message goes something like this: You might as well laugh and enjoy the total chaos that you're muddling through, because you can't really do anything about it, and anyone who thinks you can is an uptight, humorless Home Dictator who's never had any experience with real life.

Well, in my heart, I'm with the muddlers. It's more fun, and instinct tells me that the folks who tell us to just muddle through are probably coming closer to the way things really are.

But when it comes to our children, what then? On the one hand, we can't afford to just leave it to chance. And on the other hand, we all need our sense of humor more than ever. Can you have it both ways?

In this book, I say you can. You have to laugh; you have to accept that your plans are not always going to work out like clockwork. But you can have a master plan, and you can make it work.

Chapter 2

How Come the Workplace Seems So Structured and Home Seems So Chaotic?

Because there aren't any four-year-olds running around the workplace?

That *is* part of it. There's no getting around it, home is a place with a lot of loose ends, and that's as it should be. The loose ends of home are creativity, exploration, self-expression, and the fact that not everyone is working from the same mission statement. Your four-year-old's mission statement, if he could express it, would be different from yours. Your fifteen-year-old's mission statement—if she's talking to you on any given day—would certainly be different.

But perhaps that's not what makes home and the workplace so different. Everyone always has his or her agenda. Your company might have a mission statement, but unless you're one of the owners of the company, it's probably not the one you would have written up. The computer software programmer, the stock clerk, and the chief buyer in your company would probably all have different mission statements, too, if you asked them.

We all see life from our own point of view. There's a story about an actor who got a part in a Broadway play—the classic *A Streetcar Named Desire,* which starred a young Jessica Tandy and Marlon Brando. In the last scene, after Tandy's character suffers a complete mental collapse, she has to be taken to the hospital by a doctor, accompanied by two attendants. The actor was to play one of the attendants.

"I've got a part in a new play!" he told a friend. "It's all about this guy who comes to take a lady to a nuthouse."

We all tend to think of ourselves as the center of the universe, and why shouldn't we? The difference is, that actor had a director who did understand the overall picture, and every company has someone in charge who knows its central mission and knows how the computer programmer, the stock clerk, and the chief buyer fit into it.

This is what you need at home. You don't need to create a mini-dictatorship, but you do need to have one person who'll do the overall thinking, who will have a master plan and understand how everyone else fits into it. You need a CEO. And that CEO is you.

You've got all the qualifications for the job. You know all the personnel better than anyone else. You have the vision, you have the brains, you have the experience, and you have the mandate.

If you're a single mom, you're definitely the only one who's qualified. If you're part of a couple, and your husband is one of those who has woken up and discovered that we're almost in the twenty-first century, and men's and women's roles have changed . . . well, you're one of the lucky ones (fortunately, such husbands are not as rare as they once were). But you're still the one who knows how all the parts fit together. And if you take over the job of household CEO, you'll get things done the way *you* want them done.

And it doesn't matter whether you're a CEO or a waitress out in the workplace. You can still be that CEO at home, and you can still adapt workplace skills for home use.

A New Way of Organizing

The big news in the workplace over the past couple of decades has been the emergence of women as a significant force. We've had the opportunity to show what we could do, and we've done it. We've made the workplace a different place, and a better place.

Here's another big change that has occurred in the workplace over the past couple of decades. Modern management strategy has moved from a *process-oriented* workforce to a *project-oriented* workforce.

Work used to be built around a process. Big manufacturing companies made the same thing—cars, steel girders, stuffed panda bears—and people, in one way or another, were plugged into that process. You might start on the assembly line, then move up to foreman, then move up to supervisor; or you might start in an entry-level office job and move up to a higher-level executive function. But basically, you were still going to be involved with the same cars, or girders, or panda bears, as long as you worked for the company.

At home, it meant you lived in the same house, in the same neighborhood, and with the same neighbors. It meant you didn't get divorced.

Well, those days are gone forever. My own work life has bounced me around like a pinball, and I'm not unusual. Americans today average seven different careers between entry into the workforce and retirement.

The rest of our lives follows the same checkered pattern as our careers. We move around, sometimes from one part of the country to another. Sadly, we do get divorced; sometimes we remarry and create stepfamilies with special challenges of their own.

Process vs. Project

You know that younger generation? The one that's always going to the dogs? The one that doesn't stand a chance of competing in the world the way we did because they're too lazy, too unprepared, with the wrong attitude, wrong schooling, no motivation?

That younger generation, it seems, has been around for a long time. According to *The Frugal Housewife*, by Mrs. Child, written in 1832:

> The fact is, our young girls have no *home education*. When quite young, they are sent to schools where no feminine employments, no domestic habits, can be learned; and there they continue till they "come out" into the world. After this, few find any time to arrange, and make use of, the mass of elementary knowledge they have acquired; and fewer still have any leisure or taste for the inelegant, every-day duties of life.

Makes you wonder how we survived at all, doesn't it?

Well, surprise! Today's young women are great! They're educated, they're motivated, they're street-smart, they're ethical, and they really are ready to get out there and take the world by storm. Many of them will make their mark in the business world before they settle down to the "inelegant, every-day duties" of family life. Some of them will then decide to cut back on their work commitment, while others (over 50 percent) will continue to balance work and family— and to do it well. A recent study by Susan Seliger in the December/January 1998 issue of *Working Mother* magazine suggests that those mothers who stay in the workplace feel, more strongly than ever, that they can excel at work without sacrificing their home lives.

Seliger's survey found that 92 percent of *Working Mother*'s readers who responded to the survey considered themselves either "ambitious" or "highly ambitious" in the workplace, and by an overwhelming margin those ambitious women saw themselves as proud of their work and happy with their marriages and families.

Seliger points out how far we've come in this regard, from a time when even if women did work, it was considered unseemly for them to admit to anything as unladylike as ambition, because ambitious women were considered hard, cold, ruthless, single-minded. She quotes Janice Steil, professor of psychology at the Derner Institute of Advanced Psychological Studies at Adelphi University in Garden City, New York, as saying, "the old stereotype that ambitious women become more like men and lose their nurturing qualities is just not accurate."

Steil's research has shown no correlation, one way or the other, between ambition and nurturing qualities. The one simply does not get in the way of the other.

But for all their skill and ambition and nurturing qualities, it still seems that far too many young women will find themselves mired in the same routine that their mothers and grandmothers established. Too many of them will not have changed the way they manage their households, and too many of them will continue to see an increasing divergence between their sense of accomplishment in the workplace and that same sense at home.

It doesn't have to happen. A generation of women has conquered the world of business in spite of having few role models. They did it with courage and perseverance, and they have become the mentors and role models for the younger women who followed them.

So who are we to look to for our role models at home?

We don't have to look any farther than ourselves in our business lives.

Today, business strategy is centered around goals rather than routines. Here's how that works. Once you've identified a goal, you then create a project to meet that goal. That means figuring out a strategy, and putting together a team to carry out that strategy. You might need some experts for the team that aren't from your company, so you go out and bring them in for this project—you *outsource*.

Then, when the project is finished, you critique it, you improve the rough edges, and you go on to something new— new projects, new teams, new strategies, all connected to an overall master plan for the organization, but each one with its own challenges and rewards.

This new way of looking at business coincided directly with the infusion of women into the workforce. Coincidence? Maybe not. Men like hierarchies and pecking orders. Women like to get together and work things out by negotiation and cooperation, though we can crack the whip, too, when we need to.

So Why Don't We Do It at Home?

Why do we get bogged down at home, when we're so good in the workplace? Why does it all seem so . . . so routine?

Maybe it's because we've bought into a lot of myths about home. For instance:

You can't fire your family.

Well, that's true to an extent. You can't, of course. You can divorce your husband, and that happens to many of us, sadly. But you can't divorce your kids.

Sure, but what does that mean? That you're locked into a rut, an endless process?

It shouldn't. At home, you handle more personnel

changes than the human resources manager of a Fortune 500 company. Last year, your employee pool included a stubborn two-year-old; this year, he's been replaced by an energetic and inquiring three-year-old. That sulky sixteen-year-old you were closer to killing than firing seems to have taken off of her own accord, and suddenly your team has been augmented by an intelligent and responsible seventeen-year-old, and you realize it'll break your heart when she leaves the firm next year to head for college.

We hear a lot about all the different hats women wear, all the different job descriptions we have at home: accountant, buildings and grounds chief, chauffeur, cleaning woman, comptroller, day care worker, fashion consultant, gardener, guidance counselor, health care provider, judge, psychologist, repairperson, transportation supervisor, travel agent, veterinarian. We could probably add another ten jobs to the list with no trouble at all. But it's all a little condescending, isn't it? We don't need to invent all those different made-up titles to make us understand that being a mom is a varied and challenging job, or that it will keep us as busy as all get-out!

Besides, as CEO of the household, naturally it's our responsibility to make sure everything gets done, either by delegating or by doing it ourselves.

It's not making up a bunch of fake job descriptions that will make the difference in building our self-esteem, in giving us a sense of purpose, in creating a work environment at home that will be fulfilling, rewarding, and most of all, manageable. It's understanding the nature of work and the nature of management, and learning how to identify, plan, prioritize, and manage projects.

Chapter 3

So Where Do We Start?

Why not start with taking stock of yourself and your household? A good CEO needs to know two things at all times:

1. Where she wants to go.
2. Where she is now.

You don't need to know every step in between. That'll come, but it's not necessary right at the beginning.

Apple Computer is a company that revolutionized American business and American technology. Co-founder Steve Jobs has recalled that when he and his partner, Steven Wozniak, got together, all they had was a vision of a computer. They knew what they wanted it to be able to do. They knew what color it should be, what shape it should be. They knew that they wanted to call it "Apple," and that it should have a sprightly little Apple logo on it.

They didn't have the foggiest notion of how to design or

build a computer. However, they knew that they could learn all that once they had a vision.

Where you want to go is best encapsulated in a *mission statement,* and I'll discuss that shortly. But first, before you can plan your journey, you have to know where you are.

Think about how your household runs and ask yourself the following questions.

▶ What's not working?
▶ What is working?
▶ What drives you crazy?
▶ Who's doing what?

The stuff that drives you crazy is the stuff that causes fights, especially the stuff that causes the same fights over and over again. If something is not working on a more or less regular basis, then there's a faulty premise or assumption underlying it, and you really owe it to yourself to find out what it is.

Perhaps the best place to start, though, is with yourself. A good CEO knows what's going on in her company and knows the skills and limitations of all her personnel, starting with herself.

If you're like most women, right now you're doing most of what has to be done around the house. If you're a single mom, it's for darn sure you're doing almost all of it.

So, most likely, when you take the self-appraisal test below on home management skills, you'll find yourself answering "me," a whole lot more often than not, to the question "Who's doing it now?"

But let's take a look.

Self-Appraisal Test:
Home Management Skills

Activity: TIME AND TRANSPORTATION MANAGEMENT

What's it cover? Making sure everybody is where they're supposed to be, when they're supposed to be there. This means remembering on the day of the event. It also means remembering a week, and two weeks, before the event, and making sure that the family member who has to be there *knows* he has to be there.

It means knowing how he's going to get there and how he's going to get back.

And it means knowing if there are going to be conflicts—two family members having to be in two different places at the same time—and coming up with a solution.

Who does it now?

How important is it?

How important is it that I do it myself?

How I'd rate myself on a scale of 1 to 10 (10 meaning no one does it better; 1 meaning I'd have to look the word up in the dictionary):

How well is it being done now?

Activity: MONEY MANAGEMENT

What's it cover? Coming up with a family budget. Paying the bills. Planning for future expenses and large contingency expenses. Planning an investment strategy for the kids' college and your retirement. Teaching your kids how to manage money. Shopping for bargains, and planning and making large purchases.

Who does it now?

How important is it?

How important is it that I do it myself?

How I'd rate myself on a scale of 1 to 10:

How well is it being done now?

Activity: FOOD MANAGEMENT

What's it cover? Shopping for food, cooking it, and cleaning up afterwards. Planning a menu and making sure everyone eats a healthful diet.

Who does it now?

How important is it?

How important is it that I do it myself?

How I'd rate myself on a scale of 1 to 10:

How well is it being done now?

Activity: HOME MANAGEMENT

What's it cover? Cleaning, making sure there's a place for everything and everything in its place, making sure everything is in good repair, deciding when—and with what—things have to be replaced.

Who does it now?

How important is it?

How important is it that I do it myself?

How I'd rate myself on a scale of 1 to 10:

How well is it being done now?

Activity: PROPERTY MANAGEMENT

What's it cover? Care and maintenance of your house and grounds, from mowing the lawn and making sure the lawn mower is in good repair, to arranging for a new roof.

Who does it now?

How important is it?

How important is it that I do it myself?

How I'd rate myself on a scale of 1 to 10:

How well is it being done now?

Activity: HEALTH MANAGEMENT

What's it cover? Taking care of minor illnesses and deciding when it's time to go to the doctor for major ones. Making sure that basic remedies and first aid supplies are on hand. Seeing that everyone in the family gets proper rest, diet, and exercise. Making sure that everyone gets regular checkups at the doctor, the dentist, the optometrist, etc.

Who does it now?

How important is it?

How important is it that I do it myself?

How I'd rate myself on a scale of 1 to 10:

How well is it being done now?

Activity: HUMAN RESOURCES MANAGEMENT

What's it cover? Making sure everyone knows his/her responsibilities, is properly trained and motivated to do a good job, and gets the job done in a timely fashion.

Who does it now?

How important is it?

How important is it that I do it myself?

How I'd rate myself on a scale of 1 to 10:

How well is it being done now?

Activity: EDUCATION MANAGEMENT

What's it cover? Helping with homework, and staying on top of kids' schoolwork so that you know enough to make sure that they're keeping up in school. Being active in PTA activities. Home schooling, if that's your philosophy. Keeping up with your own education, either formally or informally.

Who does it now?

How important is it?

How important is it that I do it myself?

How I'd rate myself on a scale of 1 to 10:

How well is it being done now?

Activity: VACATION MANAGEMENT

What's it cover? Planning vacations and budgeting to pay for them. Making sure that the vacations are going to be pleasurable and enriching for everyone.

Who does it now?

How important is it?

How important is it that I do it myself?

How I'd rate myself on a scale of 1 to 10:

How well is it being done now?

Activity: QUALITY OF LIFE MANAGEMENT

What's it cover? Planning outings for your family that enrich them culturally or give them healthy exercise. Making sure there's time for spirituality and service—for your family and for yourself.

Who does it now?

How important is it?

How important is it that I do it myself?

How I'd rate myself on a scale of 1 to 10:

How well is it being done now?

Activity: EMERGENCY PREPAREDNESS: FAMILY

What's it cover? Getting the phone numbers of the fire department (volunteer or otherwise), local and state police, rescue squad, family doctor, poison control hot line, and any other emergency numbers that might apply to your family.

Making sure that those numbers are posted where everyone in the family can see them.

Making sure you know what the best fire exits are for every room in the house and how to get everyone out in case of an emergency. If necessary, holding fire drills periodically so that everyone else knows, too.

Who does it now?

How important is it?

How important is it that I do it myself?

How I'd rate myself on a scale of 1 to 10:

How well is it being done now?

Activity: EMERGENCY PREPAREDNESS: LEGAL

What's it cover? Making sure that you know where your insurance policies are and how to reach your insurance agent.

Making sure you know where the keys to your family's safe-deposit box are.

Making sure that your nanny, or anyone doing child care for you (including relatives), has your written permission to take your child to the hospital in case of any medical emergency.

Who does it now?

How important is it?

How important is it that I do it myself?

How I'd rate myself on a scale of 1 to 10:

How well is it being done now?

Activity: HOLIDAY AND BIRTHDAY PLANNING

What's it cover? Making sure everyone knows important dates, and making sure everyone is aware of them far enough in advance to save up for presents and plan to be available for celebrations.

Making sure that all parties and other celebrations of family events (for example, Thanksgiving dinner) are planned appropriately for everyone in the family (including you).

Who does it now?

How important is it?

How important is it that I do it myself?

How I'd rate myself on a scale of 1 to 10:

How well is it being done now

Activity: PET CARE

What's it cover? Making sure that the family pets are fed, walked, bathed, brushed, taken to the vet.

Making sure that any medications or dietary supplements prescribed for the pets are actually administered.

Making sure that pet care is provided for if the family is going out of town.

Who does it now?

How important is it?

How important is it that I do it myself?

How I'd rate myself on a scale of 1 to 10:

How well is it being done now?

Activity: (FILL IN YOUR OWN)

What's it cover?

Who does it now?

How important is it?

How important is it that I do it myself?

How I'd rate myself on a scale of 1 to 10:

How well is it being done now?

You might have other categories to add—or you might want to break down these sample categories differently. Remember, this is your list, and its purpose is to help you figure out what *your* priorities are, what you actually are spending time on, and whether this is the most productive use of your time. Once you've done this to your own satisfaction, you can begin involving the rest of your family, either by delegating responsibility or by discussing the delegation of responsibility.

As CEO of a company, you'd have a board of directors, to whom you'd take many corporate problems and corporate decisions for review. You'd present problems to them, suggest possible solutions, and arrive, after discussion, at mutually satisfactory decisions about various courses of action.

You'd also have employees, with whom you wouldn't consult. You'd give them certain responsibilities, and you'd even give them the responsibility of delegating certain responsibilities to others, but ultimately they'd be reporting back to you.

One of the big differences between a home and a corporation? In a home, the board of directors and the employees are the same people.

There are choices you present to your family-as-board-of-directors for discussion, and others that you tell your family-as-employees about. Sometimes it's easy: you don't discuss with your seven-year-old when her bedtime is going to be; you do discuss with the family whether they want to go to Disney World or Bermuda for vacation.

Of course, your family isn't really a board of directors, and your family members certainly aren't your employees. There are some choices you'll discuss with your entire family. There'll be others you'll discuss only with your husband: Will you be able to afford private school for the kids? And is that what you both want for them? And there'll be some decisions that you don't discuss with anyone—that you just make on your own.

But first, you need to sit down by yourself and figure out what *you* think about the various aspects of your home/corporation, how they're running, and how you feel about them.

Look at each category on your list and ask yourself:

How Important Is It?

Well, all these things are important. But they're important in different ways, and the differences aren't exactly the kind of differences you'd measure on a scale from 1 to 10. They're differences of degree, and they're also differences in kind. I think of them more or less in terms of movie ratings, something like this:

> **Rated R: R**eally **R**eally **R**eally important—everything will fall apart if I let this go for even one day.

In my household, making sure that the kids keep up with their homework falls into this category. So does making sure that we all take our vitamins.

> **Rated G:** I need to **G**et this done, but it can slide for a few days if necessary without anything really cataclysmic happening.

If we wait till next week to sit down and make our vacation plans for next summer, no harm will be done. Nor will it be the end of the world if we don't clean out the basement this week. Of course, you can't put these things off forever!

Rated PG: If I'm thoroughly Prepared for it, that's Good enough.

An example of a PG-rated activity would be emergency preparedness. You want to make absolutely sure that you know what to do, and that everyone in the family knows what to do, if there's a fire. You might want to have a fire drill once every six months, to make absolutely sure that everyone remembers or that nothing is blocking what used to be an exit route. But you don't have to devote time each day to dealing with it.

How Important Is It That I Do It Myself?

There are some things you have to do yourself. There are a lot of things you don't have to do yourself. Generally speaking, you know the difference.

Is stacking the dishwasher an art form that only you can master? And even if it were, how much difference does it make if it gets precisely mastered or not?

Cooking? Cleaning house? It's important that these things get done, but it doesn't really make much difference who does them. It might, in fact, be preferable that your kids and/or your husband play a major role in some of these areas.

There are other tasks that you might absolutely not want to entrust to anyone else. Who in your household is the person who decides when someone goes to school in the morning or stays home in bed? Who decides when it's time for the children's cough medicine, and when it's time to call the doctor or make a trip to the emergency room? If it's you, then it's got to be you every time.

You're the CEO, which means that it's your job to either

delegate or deal with things personally. You have to decide
what you mean by "important."

Here are the key questions:

▶ Is this something you wouldn't trust anyone else to
  do?
▶ Is it something that you just wouldn't feel right
  about unless you did it yourself?
▶ Is it something that gives you great personal pleasure
  and satisfaction?

Again, this isn't a graduated series of choices going
from the highest to lowest priority or from the best reason to
the worst. Each choice involves a complex balance sheet of
advantages and disadvantages to hands-on involvement, just
as it would in a business.

*Lately, Alison has been starting to wonder whether fixing
and freezing those nutritious meals is really worth it. Whitney is fourteen, and isn't it time she started learning to
cook for herself? Alison tries to remember at what age she
developed her love for cooking. She must have been about
Whitney's age when she first cooked a pot roast for her
father.*

*She sighs. Not much chance of Whitney's doing that.
Maybe she could fix martinis for her dad and his new trophy wife.*

*Oh, well, no need to start wallowing in bitterness. She
goes back to slicing the meat loaf and putting it in Ziploc
bags.*

Life with teenagers is tough. Half the time Alison isn't
even sure whether Whitney is eating the nutritious meals
she prepares for her, or is just dumping them and going to

McDonald's. Certainly, she's never gotten any acknowledgment or thanks from her daughter. But doing it is something that gives her personal satisfaction, and sometimes that's reason enough. Sometimes we just have to trust our instincts. Alison knows that she works her schedule around the important events in her kids' lives as much as she can, but she knows, as well, that because of her job there'll be a lot of times when she's not at home. It makes her feel good to know that she's leaving a part of herself at home in those meals.

What she doesn't know yet (because these are things we only discover later, in retrospect) is that she is creating a new family tradition.

Now it's two years later. Whitney is sixteen, and—needless to say—still a teenager. There are still the fights, and the wails of *You don't understand!* and the slammed doors, but there are some good conversations, too, and some important shared moments.

> *Alison is in the kitchen. In the morning, she has to catch a flight to Chicago, so she's getting ready to start her late-night cooking ritual for the night before a trip. It's ten o'clock. Whitney is out. She went to a movie at the mall with friends, and she has an eleven o'clock curfew. She's mostly pretty good at keeping her curfews, but still, every night about this time, Alison starts to get a little prickle of worry.*
>
> *The back doorknob turns at five minutes after ten; it's Whitney.*
>
> *"Everything okay?" Alison asks her.*
>
> *"Yeah," Whitney says noncommittally. "I just felt like coming home early, that's all. You know, Trevor has a big game day after tomorrow."*
>
> *"I know," Alison says. "And I won't be back from Chicago in time to go to it."*

Whitney smiles. "But he'll have a great meal to eat before the game, won't he?"

Alison smiles, too. "I hope so."

"What are you going to cook?"

"Well, I don't know. Do you have any suggestions?"

"You know, Mom, I heard about this sweet new recipe for veggie burgers. Way healthy, way delicious. I bet we could make them together . . ."

If something makes you feel actively good about doing it, it's probably a good thing. But the same might not be true of those things that you "just wouldn't feel right about" unless you did them yourself. If your household isn't running smoothly and you feel swamped all the time, maybe it's because you have too many things that you "just wouldn't feel right about" unless you did them yourself. Maybe some of the voices that are telling you it's just not right unless you do it yourself are not your own.

Peg is thinking about the talk she had with Mike earlier this morning, and the words he left her with.

She has an appointment to talk with the guidance counselor at Vincent's school, and she has to take off two hours after lunch to do it. This is one of those mornings when she's thanking her lucky stars for Alison—she understands what it's like, and she'll give Peg the time she needs, as long as she makes up the work.

But she's still feeling disgruntled. She's not looking forward to the meeting, and she let it be known at breakfast—her breakfast, his supper.

"Hey, if you wanted me to do it, why didn't you say so?" Mike asked her. "Or you could have set it up in the morning, so I could have gone with you."

Peg goes over the possibilities.

Would she trust Mike to do it? Well, certainly he'd

show up for the appointment. He's always reliable about that sort of thing. But would he ask the right questions? Could she trust him to do that?

Oh, come on, Peg, you're getting a little obsessive here, aren't you? she asks herself with a laugh. As though Vincent's entire future hung in the balance of what this guidance counselor says in this one conference. When she comes home, she'll tell Mike what the guidance counselor said, and they'll talk it through, and evaluate it, and see how it applies to what they already know about their son. Then they'll talk to Vincent, and to the guidance counselor again, if necessary.

If Mike went, he wouldn't repeat every word that the counselor said, but as they talked for a while, he'd get out all the important points.

So . . . yes, she could probably trust Mike to do it, so it has to be the other option. Somehow, she just wouldn't feel right unless she did it herself.

Isn't that a little silly? she asks herself. You trust Mike to do what needs to be done. What do you mean, you just wouldn't feel right?

Basically, what we often mean by *I just wouldn't feel right,* and what Peg came to realize that she meant here, is that we wouldn't feel right not being at the center of something this important.

That's the right instinct. As CEOs of our families, we should be at the center of important decisions and situations. But being project manager is not the same thing as doing every task in the project, which is what Peg came to realize. She would take charge of the project of getting Vincent back on track, but Mike and Vincent would both do their share.

How Would I Rate Myself on a Scale of 1 to 10?

This calls for honest self-appraisal; you're not answering for anyone except yourself. Are you prepared for any contingency? Do you really have a given task under control, or are you constantly scrambling to keep up? Do you approach the task with confidence—whether you enjoy it or not—or do you approach it with a sense of dread?

Setting Priorities

Now that you've finished answering these questions, it's time to set your priorities.

The things that you're good at it, that are really important, and that you really ought to be handling yourself—well, it's not rocket science to figure out that you'll be handling these things yourself, that you'll place a high priority on them, and that they will represent an efficient and productive use of your time.

You might, for example, determine that education management is a highest-priority item. You've decided that the difference between a great education for your kids and a mediocre one, between a top college and the local community college—or between a high school education and being the first in your family to finish college—depends on what kind of support system your kids have, and you believe that support system can't come only from within the school. You believe that this support has to come from active and concerned parents whose involvement in the educational process will provide a role model for your kids, and you love doing it—you love teaching little children their numbers, and you love discussing history and current events with junior high-age kids.

Then education management is going to be time well spent. It's going to be maximum-return time, and you'll want to make sure you allot it to yourself.

What about an item that is high priority, that you know you ought to be doing yourself, but you don't rank yourself very high in the skills department?

Let's take money management. You firmly believe that if your family is going to have the kind of budget that will enable it to achieve the goals that you—and your family—value the most, then you're going to have to make that budget work. Only trouble is, you've never been very good at it.

Well, if you have to do it, then you'll have to learn to be good at it. That doesn't mean you can't get help.

You'd do it at work. You'd identify the problem, you'd put a team together, and you'd come up with a solution. You can do the same at home. You can sit down with an accountant and have him show you how to organize a budget, you can sit down with someone who knows a little more about computers than you do and have her show you how to use a home and office finance management program. You can sit your kids down with you once a month and have them sort receipts out into piles so that you can enter them into your computer.

What about a task that's not the highest priority in the world but you're really good at it, and you love to do it? For me, if something breaks—a beautiful vase or a plate—I don't want to send it out to be repaired. To take something beautiful and broken, and make it whole again . . . I don't count it as time away from something more important. To me it *is* important.

Make sure that there are places for tasks like that in your schedule, too. You deserve them.

And, finally, what about the tasks that you're not crazy

about, that don't require your personal touch, that are outside your area of expertise, and that can be entrusted to
someone else without fear that things will fall apart? For
me, it's a task like changing the oil in the car. You might
love working on cars, while gluing a vase might leave you
cold.

Very few of us would ever say, "I just love stacking and
emptying the dishwasher, and nobody else can do it the way
I can."

What would you do in business? You'd identify these
tasks and delegate them. And if there wasn't anyone within
the organization that you could delegate a task to, or if you
felt that household personnel resources were better used
elsewhere, you'd *outsource* it.

Here are some examples (these may not apply to your
family, but they'll give you a general idea):

Tasks to delegate within the family: Keeping the family room picked up, stacking and unloading the dishwasher, washing the car.

*Tasks to outsource because no one in the organization
can do it:* Dry cleaning, replacing drains and gutters,
locksmith work.

*Tasks to outsource because you'd prefer to utilize
family personnel for other things:* Changing the oil in
the car, getting tickets and reservations for a trip.

Tasks to outsource if you're really busy. You don't
have to be a business to hire someone else to pay your
bills and keep your books for you—there are people
who'll do this for a reasonable fee.

Outsourcing is one of the hot new concepts in the business world today. In fact, some business savants are saying

that it's just the beginning of a vast new trend—that in the corporation of the future, everything will be outsourced. There will be no corporation of the future as we know it— just project-based attachments among various outsourcing modules.

That's the way they talk in the business world, which is one of the reasons why we love being home, with real human beings who speak real English and say things like "Mommy, it's not fair! It's Alec's turn to take out the garbage!"

But the point is: when is the last time you heard about a hot new trend in the home? It just doesn't happen. If there are discussions of trends at all, they're negative ones. People bemoan the disappearance of older, traditional values, like families sitting down and eating together (a trend that could come back again, with proper management). The traditional view of the home is, well, traditional. Trends need not apply.

And this is, for the most part, good stuff. We keep traditional values because they've proved their worth. But that doesn't mean we can't, at the same time, be open to new ideas that have also proved their worth.

So what about outsourcing?

Of course, it's not a totally new idea. If there are termites in the basement, we don't think twice about calling in a professional exterminator.

But too often we can't help listening to voices that are inside our heads, or coming from sources close to us. Those are the voices that say: *You're not being a real mom if you don't do all these things yourself. You're not as good as your mother was, or your grandmother. What's wrong with you? Don't you love your family enough?*

These aren't issues in the workplace, not even in a family business. And they shouldn't be issues at home, either.

Project Manager: Helene Kuchera, thirty-five, human resources manager for a regional telephone company. Married, mom of Sam, eight, Walt, seven, and Billy, five.

I went out with David for five years before I married him—we started dating in high school—so I was over at his folks' house a lot, and Maggie, his mom, always seemed to be doing laundry (David was one of five boys). This was never a problem for her. She seemed to like doing the laundry, and she was always talking about it when she did it. "Laundry's one thing you have to do yourself if you want it done right," she always said. And she'd show me, if I happened to be there, just what you did for a bloodstain, or a grape juice stain, or what to do with collars so they wouldn't wear out so fast. What do you do? I'm not quite sure, because I wasn't that good a learner.

But what I did learn was this: laundry is important, and you can't expect it to be done right unless you do it yourself.

I learned that so well that I just gave a super-high priority to laundry without even thinking about it—not only important, but important that I do it myself.

I knew there were still too many things that I was setting aside for myself to do, assuming that I had to do them or they wouldn't get done right, that I had to do them or I was being irresponsible, that if I didn't do them I wasn't fulfilling my responsibilities as a wife and a mother.

I don't know how many times I looked at that list before I realized, *I don't have to do laundry!*

Well, it wasn't easy. But I started sending it out, and the world didn't come to an end. If there was a difference in how white things got, I certainly didn't notice it. And neither, I discovered, did David. After a while, I even got bold enough to tell him I was doing it, and I found out that he didn't care. From there, it was a hop, skip, and jump to asking him to share the dropping it off and picking it up with me, and now . . . well, it's a small thing, but it's made a huge difference in my being able to manage things in the house.

How Well Is It Being Done Now?

This is a trickier question than it sounds. The classic answer is, "If it ain't broke, don't fix it." That's the simple way of approaching this particular issue. Deal with the problems that need solutions; don't worry about the things that are taking care of themselves.

Basically, this is a good idea. You can drive yourself nuts trying to micromanage.

Peg learned about micromanagement when Vincent was twelve. She had instituted a rule about putting clothes away, and it was important to her. She believed that you learn good habits when you're young and that a neat house breeds a neat mind.

Peg had rebelled when she was twelve, too. She picked nothing up.

Finally, her mother told her, "If you don't start picking up, I'm going to throw away your room."

"You can't throw away my room," Peg said.

It turned out that she could, and did. Peg came home from school three days later to find her room stripped bare. The only things that had been left in it were the things that were in order, which meant virtually nothing. She ran downstairs in a fit of indignation.

"You did it! You threw my room away!"

"It's all out in the garbage," her mother said. "If you hurry, you should be able to get it back. They don't pick the garbage up till tomorrow morning."

Peg slipped back into her old habits fairly quickly, until one day, about three months later, she came home from school, and . . .

"I CAN'T BELIEVE YOU THREW MY ROOM AWAY AGAIN!" she screamed at her mother.

"She didn't," said Colleen, her oldest sister. "I did."

That was the end of Peg's flirtation with messiness.

When Vincent was twelve, she was working on him to fold his laundry and put it away. He wasn't getting it.

"Take it easy," Mike told her. "He's putting his clothes away."

"He's wadding them up and stuffing them in his drawers! Any old drawer! He's not folding anything."

Peg couldn't stand it. One day, she pulled everything out of the drawers and dumped all the clothes on Vincent's bed, intending to confront him when he got home.

"Mom, what is this?" he asked, seriously hurt. "Why are you going through all my things? Do you think I'm on drugs?"

"No, I don't think anything like that, Vincent," she said.

"Then why are you going through my things?"

"I wasn't going through your things. You just have to start arranging them neatly in your drawers."

"Why? I know where things are. If I want to find a pair of clean underpants, or a pair of blue socks, I can find them. My room is neat. Why would anybody care what the inside of my dresser drawers looked like unless they wanted to snoop through them?"

Peg came to accept that this was an issue that did not matter profoundly. It wasn't broke; it didn't really need to be fixed.

But this is not always the case. Things don't take care of themselves. As CEO, sometimes it's your job, when something ain't broke, to ask, "Why not? How does it happen that it ain't broke? And how sure am I that it's going to stay not broke?" Is only one person able to make this run smoothly, or is there a backup plan?

I have a friend named Bill who bought a beautiful old

farmhouse in the country. It had been remodeled over the years, and the electric service had been added to gradually. The first week they were there, his thirteen-year-old stepson, who was interested in things like that, tried out all the circuit breakers. This drove my friend and his wife nuts for about half a day, but in the long run it turned out to be a good thing, because Shane knew which breaker controlled which outlet, and he would run down to the basement and fix the problem.

That, however, was the intermediate long run. In the long long run, Shane went off to college.

The first week he was gone, Bill realized that there were parts of the house that he didn't use often, like the back porch and the attic, that had light switches he couldn't find. There were lights he couldn't turn on. There were lights he couldn't turn off. He had to call Shane at his dorm to get instructions on how to find the switches.

The real fun, however, came when a circuit breaker blew. Bill took a flashlight and went down to the basement. Everything was neatly labeled, but the labels were all in code. What was "TC4K"? Where was "LM3@J5"?

"Hi, this is Shane. I'm not in right now, but . . ."

"Shane, it's your dad. All the lights in our bedroom are out. How do I find the circuit breaker?"

Shane called back about three hours later.

"Hi, Dad. *All* the lights?"

"Well, the electric clock is still on, and the TV still works."

"So it's the light over your bed, and the air conditioner. Okay, that's easy. Look for a breaker labeled 'GE2MR.' "

" 'GE2MR' . . . got it. But just out of curiosity, why did you label it that?"

"Well, it's a GE air conditioner, and it's the second one we have. GE1 is the air conditioner in my room. Not that I think my room is more important or anything, it's just that I labeled it first. MR is Mom's room. Anyway, gotta run. Good luck."

And, half an hour later:

"Hi, this is Shane. I'm not in right now, but . . ."

"Shane, it's your dad again. There is no breaker marked 'GE2MR.' "

And, well after midnight . . .

"Dad, hope I didn't wake you. Did you try the breaker box in the front of the basement or the breaker box in the back of the basement?"

"What breaker box in the back of the basement . . . ?"

Project Manager: Linda Haverick, thirty-five, receptionist. Remarried (Bill), mom of Jason, seventeen, and Lindsey, fourteen (first marriage); Donna, eight, and Deanna, six (second marriage).

We never all seemed to eat together. There was never a meal, except for Christmas or Thanksgiving, when the whole family sat down at the table together.

This wasn't something we'd planned. On the other hand, it wasn't something anyone ever complained about, either. But even if it wasn't a problem, it didn't feel quite right. It wasn't the way I'd been brought up, and I missed my family meals.

I didn't say anything about it for a long time. But one Thanksgiving, as we were giving blessings for the family's being together, Donna said, "It's so special when we're *all* together."

I grabbed the opportunity. I started telling stories about Sunday dinners when I was little, and how the whole family would get involved with my homework, or we'd talk about sports, or books we'd read, or movies we'd seen.

"Sure," said Jason. "I can just see trying to talk about a Chris Farley movie at a Sunday dinner."

Bill stepped in at that point, bless his heart. "I don't know," he said. "I'd actually like to know more about what you guys are watching and listening to. Doesn't mean I won't give my opinion about it."

"Yeah, but Sunday dinner? I've generally got stuff to do on Sundays. And I don't see you giving up the Bengals for it."

"I could do Friday dinners," said Lindsey quietly.

The two little ones were all for it.

"I guess I could do Fridays," said Jason.

"There's one part of that old family tradition I don't want to continue," I said. "That's the part where Mom did all the work. Everyone's going to help with dinner—and with the cleanup afterward."

"I knew there was a catch," said Jason. But he was grinning.

So that's how we started having Friday night dinner together. I'm not saying we didn't have a great family before, and I'm not saying that the kids would have gone to hell in a handbasket if we hadn't started doing it. But things are nicer this way.

As I've said before, if something's running smoothly and you're doing it, that doesn't mean it couldn't run just as smoothly with someone else doing it. Fix the things that are broken first. But don't forget to be aware of the things that aren't. Frequently they can be the difference between a great CEO and one who's never quite on top of things and can't quite understand why she isn't.

Part II

Identifying Projects

Chapter 4

What's a Project?

A project is a unit of work that has a beginning, a middle, and an end. It comes about in response to a goal, a situation, or a problem that you can generally foresee. You can plot a strategy for completing a project, you can assign personnel and resources to it, and you can analyze it when it's over.

Beyond that, a project is what you make it. And this is where your skill as CEO comes to the fore, because no two businesses are the same, and no two households are the same. Identifying, designing, and seeing projects through to completion is an art.

Projects can be large or small, complex or simple. They can cover long periods of time or they can be finished quickly. If you have a complicated, long-term project, you can break it down to projects within projects.

The point is, you can do it—using your common sense as well as your business sense. Whether you've been a secretary or a CEO in the business world, you've used your knowledge of how things work to make things work better, and you've done a darn good job of it. You can do the same thing at home. And, equally important, doing it will give you that sense of control and competence.

Control and competence. Two words that fit together but are so hard to bring together. How often have all of us thought: How can I ever get my life under control when everyone around me is so incompetent?

It does seem that way, doesn't it? If you get three women together to discuss anything from Shakespeare to world hunger to computer marketing strategies for the Pacific Rim, at some point in the discussion (generally fairly early on) they'll be trading combat stories about what they have to endure on the home front.

One of them will tell the story about the husband who said he'd take care of the shopping. Arriving home with a twenty-pound ValuPak of hamburger, he promptly stuck in the freezer, so that by the time his spouse found it, it had been permafrosted into one solid chunk, unusable for anything except perhaps the cornerstone of a building.

Another one will have a story about the fifteen-year-old whose basketball team was going to the county finals, and who announced to her mother at breakfast the day of the game that, by the way, the team would be coming over for a pregame snack at around five, and oh, yes, she needed a new pair of sneakers for the game—which wouldn't have been so much of a problem except that Mom already had a dentist's appointment for that morning and another kid who had to be driven to a Little League game that afternoon at five.

And the third will chime in with a story about going out in a sleeting February morning to drive to work, only to find that her baby-sitter had taken the car the night before and brought it back with the gas tank empty.

You'll start to notice a familiar rising edge to the voices

of all these women, and a familiar theme will quickly develop: why is everyone in the world an idiot except us?

They aren't really. But it really seems that way a lot of the time, doesn't it? That's because they tend not to think like us at exactly those moments when, if they did follow the plan we have laid out in our minds, everything would work perfectly.

This is one of the key reasons why so many women find themselves tempted to stay late at the office or to take an extra assignment on top of an already full workload. Because at the office, there's a plan that's designed from the top and communicated to everyone.

Once you're used to that kind of order and structure, with things working most of the time and clear accountability, it's really hard to come back to a place where things don't work because everyone around you seems to be willfully dedicated to making them not work.

And that's when things start to spin out of control and life starts to seem like an endless expanse of frustration.

Endless tasks are doomed to frustration. But if parts of them are separated out and turned into manageable projects, then nothing has to be endless and you can be the project manager of your home.

Defining a Manageable Project

Basically, a manageable project is one that you can break down into the following components:

- ▶ A goal
- ▶ A strategy for success
- ▶ Tactics and implementation
- ▶ A timetable
- ▶ Step-by-step review

► Celebration of success
► Overall review

Okay, let's take a look at this with a real project and a project manager who made it work.

Project Manager: Kelly McIver, thirty-eight, motel manager. Married, mom of Eric, fourteen, Danny, nine, and Traci, five.

I wasted time, energy, and money in going back and forth to the supermarket two or three times a week—or even more during particularly difficult weeks. It used to drive me nuts, until I realized that just because I'd been doing it the same way for years, that didn't mean I had to keep doing it that way forever.

I knew that I didn't want to keep going back to the store, and I planned my week's shopping accordingly. That is to say, according to my plans, we should have made it through a whole week at a time.

You know how it was. I'd tell my husband to pick up the meat from the butcher's, and instead of the rump roast that I'd been counting on for our Friday night dinner guests, he'd pick up a chuck roast.

"What the heck is this?" I'd say.

He'd be pleased as a puppy. "Hey, isn't that a great piece of meat?" he'd say. "And it was cheaper. Good buy, huh?"

Yeah. As in good-bye, honey, I'm heading out for a trip I didn't want to make to the butcher shop to pick up the cut of meat I wanted.

Then there was always the classic case of the missing peanut butter. "What do you mean I can't have a peanut butter sandwich for my school lunch? I have to have peanut butter!"

"There isn't any peanut butter. What did you do, take a bath in it? I had a whole jar two days ago. You couldn't have eaten it all."

"Of course I didn't. I was out skateboarding with the guys and we stopped over here for some peanut butter sandwiches. I was going to mention it to you, but I guess I forgot."

So there I was, going back and forth to the grocery store two or three times a week. Not only was it a tremendous waste of time, but it took away from time I'd planned to spend doing other things. And on top of that, I'd have to take the kids with me.

You know what happens then. It's going to be even more time-consuming, and worse, you're almost certain to end up buying at least a couple of things that weren't on your list, because the kids have begged you, or else you'll end up stopping at McDonald's on the way home and blowing the money you saved buying paper towels and canned soup at the warehouse club on Happy Meals as a reward for their being good.

Kelly is someone I met at a seminar I was giving on women and home management. She was talking about a problem I've encountered myself, and I don't think I know anyone with kids who hasn't. American mothers go to the store with their children on an average of 2.7 times per week, and it can make the difference between a manageable food line on your budget and one that threatens to devour the whole thing. You feel rushed, frenzied, harried, one step behind and never likely to catch up—out of control.

That was the way the Kelly felt. "It just feels like there's nothing I can do," she told me.

"What if this was a problem of communication with your staff about purchasing supplies for your motel?" I asked her. "Would you think there was nothing you could do?"

"If I did, I'd be fired," she said. "But no, of course not. If this was a problem at work, I would never have let it get this far out of hand."

"What would you have done?" I asked.

We sat down and worked on the problem as a project.

Kelly's Project

THE GOAL: To meet all my shopping needs for a week in one trip to the store. To save time and to save money.

(Neale's note: a goal should be simple. Kelly stated three goals, but it's really only one goal. If Kelly meets all her shopping needs in one trip to the store, that in itself will save her time and money.)

THE STRATEGY: To do it myself this week, so as to get the process clear in my mind, and then to standardize the process and involve the whole family.

THE TACTICS:

FIRST STEP: to plan all the major meals for the week. This means I need to have a pretty good idea of who is going to be home and whether we are having guests over on any night.

(Neale's note: This is actually not so hard. Speaking for myself, I'd rather plan meals for a week, where you get a certain amount of overview—you're only going to eat so much red meat, you'll have a pasta night, a vegetarian night, a night of leftovers—than go into a panic every afternoon around five.)

SECOND STEP: to have a general sense of breakfasts, lunches, and healthy snacks that would be eaten at home or carried to school or work during the course of the week, and the ingredients that would go into them.

THIRD STEP: to allow for contingencies. There has to be a plan for extra meals or last-minute dinner guests. There also has to be a plan for kids, husbands, or even myself being unexpectedly absent for an evening. A total strategy ensures that there's enough to go around in the former case, and not too many perishables that might go to waste in the latter case.

FOURTH STEP: to check on what staples need to be replenished, and stock up on them.

THE TIMETABLE: One week. I knew there was nothing in this project that I shouldn't be able to do, on my own and for myself, in that amount of time.

THE STEP-BY-STEP REVIEW: I had the list of meals I'd planned up on the refrigerator, and I could check them off as I went along. I could keep mental track of how much was being used and how close the reality was to the schedule, just as I would have done at work. As long as things are running smoothly, that's enough, if you're a decent manager and have half a head on your shoulders—which, most days, I do.

I used a little extra diligence on items like peanut butter that I knew could disappear quickly without warning. You know what the potential trouble spots in your organization are—they should never catch you by surprise. I would never run out of computer diskettes or fax paper at the office.

As it turned out, there was a run on bread and peanut butter that week, and I was prepared for it. A trip to the warehouse club to stock up, and there's bread in the freezer, and always two backup jars of peanut butter.

THE CELEBRATION OF SUCCESS: Chocolate is always a good choice for a celebration of success. I had my quiet celebration on Sunday night, just me and Lady Godiva.

OVERALL REVIEW: At the end of the week, I was on top of everything, and I was ready to start phase two of this operation.

One good thing I realized about planning meals in advance is that you can plan which ones you're going to cook yourself and which ones someone else is going to be responsible for.

Half the Battle

But all of this was only half of Kelly's battle. She was shopping for food and household items more efficiently than she had been, but this still was not something that gave her great personal satisfaction, nor was it something that she, and she alone, was capable of doing. Nor, for that matter, was it something that would send the world crashing to a halt if there were some screwups during a transition period.

So here was her next project.

Note that this is a *new* project, not just more of the same old same old. Life goes on, in the home just as at work, and there are always new problems to be solved. But this next project is a different project. It has different goals, it requires different skills and strategies, and it makes a difference if you think about it this way.

Kelly's Project #2

THE GOAL: To insure that all my family's shopping needs for a week are met in one trip to the store, not necessarily by me. To continue to save time and money.

THE STRATEGY: To standardize the process so that anyone can do it.

(Neale's note: This is the center of the whole concept of project management. You know what you want, and you know it's not brain surgery. So all you have to do is find a simple way of making it clear to everyone else.)

THE TACTICS:

FIRST STEP: Make a list of everything that gets bought on a regular basis. This list has to be very complete and very detailed. If I tell my husband to buy blue cheese dressing, chances are he'll come back with a gallon of lobster remoulade Caribbean smoky ranch-style dressing. But if I write down on a list, "Eight-ounce bottle of Marie's blue cheese dressing. Round glass bottle, find in produce section," there's a much better chance that he'll get exactly that.

Why should I have to write all that down? Because it only takes a minute, and it gets me what I want, which saves a whole lot of time later on.

It's best to just accept that this is how it is. I use Charmin plain white extrasoft toilet paper in the medium-size rolls, so they'll fit my holders. My mother uses Great Northern, and she likes it with a little blue floral print. If she asks me to pick up some toilet paper, I know exactly what kind of tissue to buy. But that doesn't mean that my husband doesn't have to be told what kind of tissue he uses every day.

SECOND STEP: Once you know how to make an entry on a list, get down to making up the whole list, and don't do it alone. The whole point of this step is to make sure it's the same process for everyone in the family. I brought my husband and my kids, even the little one, in for a kitchen training session. Little ones are great for this sort of thing, because even though they can't quite do it all themselves yet, they love procedure, and they take over a lot of the job of nagging the others to do it.

We buy some stuff week after week, so I had a pad made up with all those items printed at the top. Any copy shop can do it. If you can have a reminder pad with Garfield on the top, why not have one with something useful?

I organized the list by storage space. This is what we need. This is where it's stored. This is when it should be replenished so that we don't run out of it. We want *one backup box* of dishwashing detergent, so when you use the *next-to-last box,* make sure you check it on the list. We need *two backup packages* of toilet paper, so when you *open* the third-to-last package, check that on the list.

One of the neat things about doing this job with the whole family is that you find out things you might not have known otherwise, like:

"And we need to have two boxes of oatmeal on hand."

"You know, I'm not that crazy about oatmeal. I'd rather have Cream of Wheat."

"Okay, Cream of Wheat it is. But why didn't you mention anything, given that I've been buying oatmeal for the past two years?"

"Um, I dunno."

THIRD STEP: You take the whole family shopping together. If there are items you're particular about, make sure that everyone understands the selection process. This is how you pick a melon, this is how you pick an avocado, this is how you choose meat.

Suppose they don't get the hang of it?

How much do you care? If this were something you were incredibly protective of, you wouldn't be trying to get the rest of your family to share the responsibility for it. And it's just as likely that one of them will turn out to be better than you.

Have everyone carry a notebook and take notes. How else are they going to remember? That's what I do at the motel if I'm training someone new.

Make sure everyone knows that the job doesn't end with shopping. When you get home, you'll all be putting everything away together.

FOURTH STEP: Once you've all done this together, start working on making sure everyone can do it separately. My five-year-old isn't going to do the shopping alone, but she helps to double-check and make sure the staples list is up-to-date, which makes her feel involved. My fourteen-year-old is old enough to shop for groceries if he's old enough to go to the mall, and the nine-year-old can go with him. We live in a safe neighborhood, and it's a bike ride to the supermarket. They leave the boxes at the store for me to pick up, and I pay for the groceries then. My husband certainly can handle the job, which means I'm now down to shopping once every three weeks, which is just often enough that I can keep a hands-on control of the structure without getting bogged down in doing all the work.

(Neale's note: A trip to the store, if it's planned right, can be an educational experience for your small children— or, in the language of Mom, Inc., a training experience for your newest personnel. Here are a few educational games you can play with them:

The Five Dollar Game: What will five dollars buy? Have them go to various parts of the store and find out how many of an item they can buy for five dollars: how many pounds of hamburger, how many boxes of cereal, how many bananas, how much soda, how many bags of dog food. This is an excellent way to get children comfortable with arithmetic and to start giving them a sense of what things cost—of the relative value of money.

The Change-Making Game: Once they get the hang of the Five Dollar Game—a package of lamb chops costs three dollars, so you can get one package with your five dollars, but you can't get two—have them figure out what change you would get back from five dollars. These games work especially well if you play shopping and counting games at home before you go to the store.

The Coupon Game: Have your children go through coupons in the supermarket flyers and identify products you actually use. They can cut them out and put them in an envelope to take to the store. Then have them figure out how much you'll save by using them at the store, by subtracting the value of the coupon from the price of the item.)

THE TIMETABLE: I gave myself four to six weeks to train my group, and I proved to myself that as family CEO, I'm a pretty good judge of my personnel. By the end of that period, my husband and my sons were capable of shopping on their own, and everyone was keeping track of what they used, so now no one has to go back to the store a second time during the course of a week.

THE STEP-BY-STEP REVIEW: At the end of the week, I reviewed what we'd done and what we still had to get right. Because I knew I was giving myself four to six weeks, I didn't freak out if everything wasn't shipshape at the end of the first week.

THE CELEBRATION OF SUCCESS: On week six, when the boys were off shopping, I took myself to the beauty parlor and got the works, even a manicure. And of course, I gave the family a reward of the best dinner out that McDonald's had to offer. After that, it was back to business as usual, except that I started finding productive use for that extra time. The real family celebration came later, with a trip to Disney World that I paid for with crafts I'd made and sold when I wasn't doing the shopping.

Does this sound like too much? It almost always does when you write it out. Sometimes these things are easier to do than to read about or to write about.

Maybe this particular example isn't for you. If your kitchen is *your kitchen,* and you don't want anyone else in it; if you have a sensual, spiritual connection to all aspects of food buying and preparation, then you're not going to want to train other people to share the responsibility.

But if it sounds like too much just because, well, people don't do things that way, then you might want to think about it a little more. People do things very much this way in the office. And why is that? Because in the office, the focus is on getting things done. Making things run faster, and better, than other companies in the same line of business. While at home, the focus is on . . . what?

It's not *just* on getting things done. When there's a human element—a child with a problem at school, a husband suffering from depression and self-doubt, a butterfly or a sunset to show to a four-year-old—we know that things that need doing can take a backseat.

We do know what's important. We simply do not have to worry that if we start organizing our households so that they run better, we will suddenly forget how to run outside with a little one to watch a rainbow or a sunset, or how to stop everything (remembering as a reflex action to turn off the heat under the corn on the cob) and take a sobbing teenager in our arms.

In fact, it's the most humane companies that run most efficiently, because the CEOs and managers of those companies know when to be humane and when to be efficient, and they know that the two aren't mutually exclusive.

And that, when you get right down to it, is all you have to know.

The rest of it is just a matter of finding ways that work for you.

Chapter 5

The Regular Chores

I said in the last chapter that if your kitchen is your spiritual center, and you don't want anyone else in it, you have a right to keep it that way. But at the same time, you really ought to be making sure that everyone in the household has some familiarity with all the regular chores that make a house run.

This is another way in which you're executing your power as a CEO. You have a business that has a limited basic staff, and a lot of jobs that are the functions of a generalist, not a specialist. The best way to make sure the business will be able to go on functioning smoothly, even when key personnel (which generally means you) are out of commission, is to have backup.

You know all those commercials in which Mom is sick and the whole household falls apart? Those delightful, cute little scenes featuring epic spills of gooey substances, water overflowing in sinks, eggs being cooked into small rocks in the stove. You remember how cute they are?

What's that? They're not cute at all? No, come to think of it, they're not. They're generally some ad boy's wretched idea of cute, and they're generally for some cold remedy, which is guaranteed to get Mom back on her feet in no time, taking care of this cuddly bunch of incompetents.

No. Part of your job description, as CEO, is to make sure that you've got a trained, competent, confident workforce so that this doesn't happen.

Here are the areas where anyone and everyone in your family ought to be able to step in and do at least an okay job.

Weekly Chores

Food (for anyone thirteen or over)
▶ Shopping for food, putting it away
▶ Preparing simple meals
▶ Preparing school lunches
▶ Doing dishes, cleaning up kitchen
▶ Throwing out expired food

Transportation (for those in the family who have driver's licenses)
▶ Making sure the car has gas in it (even those under driving age should know how to pump gas)
▶ Knowing how to get to any of the basic places that need to be gotten to—stores, schools, soccer practice, doctor's and dentist's offices, etc.

Cleaning (for anyone nine or over)
▶ Picking things up and knowing where to put them
▶ Knowing how to look at a room and recognize that things *haven't* been picked up
▶ Vacuuming
▶ Taking out the trash (if you recycle, this should include understanding the theory and practice of recycling—what gets sorted and where it goes)

▶ Knowing what all cleaning supplies are and what they're used for
▶ Making sure you don't run out of any cleaning supplies

Laundry (for anyone nine or over)
▶ Knowing how to sort laundry
▶ Knowing how much is too much to put in one load
▶ Knowing how much detergent (bleach, fabric softener, etc.) to use
▶ Knowing how to fold laundry
▶ Knowing at least where all your own clothes go, and having a place to put other family members' clothes so that they can put them away
▶ Knowing how to read labels; knowing what you send out to laundries or dry cleaners, knowing how to get it together to send out, and knowing where to send it to
▶ Knowing what needs to be hand-washed and how to hand-wash it

Does this seem like a lot to ask? You're really supposed to expect every member of your family to be able to do all this?

But you know it's not a lot, because you do it, and in fact, it's only a small portion of what you do. You do it because you're used to it and because being capable, efficient, and organized is just a part of you.

You do all of it because you have to and because you're used to doing it. That's why anyone would do it. People get accustomed to doing something, and become good at doing something, by doing it. That holds true for everyone in your family, not just you.

Here are some other areas—monthly or seasonal chores—where anyone and everyone in your family ought to be able to step in and do at least a passable job.

Yard and outdoor work
- ▶ Knowing all the chores that have to be done at each season (for everyone six or over—everyone should know what has to be done each spring, summer, fall, and winter, even if they're not big enough or strong enough to do all those chores yet)
- ▶ Knowing where screens and storm windows are kept, which ones go on which windows, and when you put them up (for everyone thirteen or over)
- ▶ Knowing how to rake leaves, and what a satisfactory job is—how a well-raked yard looks (for everyone nine or over). Use this same standard for snow shoveling—everyone in your family who's old enough to shovel a walk should know the dimensions of that walk.
- ▶ Knowing how to cut grass, trim hedges, *and* knowing that maintaining and putting away the tools is part of this job
- ▶ Knowing how to weed; knowing the difference between weeds and flowers or vegetables
- ▶ Knowing how to water the lawn or garden: how much is enough and how much is too much

Emergency issues
- ▶ Health emergencies—knowing the phone numbers for doctor, ambulance, emergency services, poison control center
- ▶ Fire—knowing where emergency fire exits are, and knowing that getting out of the house safely is the number-one priority.
- ▶ Auto safety—knowing how to change a flat. Knowing what auto services and road services your family has and how to reach them.
- ▶ Around the house: if there's a power failure, knowing how to check the circuit breakers, knowing where the candles are kept. If a pipe bursts, knowing

how to turn off the water—and how to reach the plumber.

Is it your job to make sure everyone knows all this stuff—and all the other stuff that you might want to add to these lists?

Yes. It's one of your key jobs as CEO.

Don't forget, being a CEO isn't all power lunches and buccaneering takeover bids. Come to think of it, all the businesses I've ever run—all the businesses that have been run by women I've known—have been noticeably short on power lunches and buccaneering takeovers.

A family is a *small* business. And a small business is not an assembly line. It's not teams of high-powered specialists.

But if you do it right, it will lead to a happier, more efficiently run household of shared responsibilities and more productive time for everyone.

We women are particularly well qualified to create this kind of work environment. Our management style at work—which, too often, we forget to bring back into the home—has changed the workplace by creating more cooperative working conditions than those that are created by male CEOs, according to any number of studies. We're collaborative rather than hierarchical, we share rewards and credit as well as distributing work equally. We have that moral authority that comes from our basic fairness.

Of course, these rules should be modified by common sense—for example, members of your family who are physically impaired aren't going to be asked to do chores that they can't do; you'll figure out together what their role will be.

Chapter 6

The *Gotcha!* Chronicles

Emotional relationships are the big difference between the workplace and home.

The people at home are the people we love most in the world—which means that they're the people with the greatest power to hurt us, infuriate us, and bring us to tears or to the brink of nervous collapse. They're the ones we'll forgive when we wouldn't forgive anyone else, and they're the ones we can be the most intransigent toward, too.

How can we treat them the same way we'd treat people we deal with in the business world?

We can't, of course. But we can treat *situations* in comparable ways. We can pay attention to the problem-solving techniques we've used and learned and developed in the business world.

When Kelly McIver told her story in a workshop I conducted, the responses she got were instructive. When she came to the line about her husband bringing home the lobster remoulade Caribbean smoky ranch-style dressing, there were chuckles.

When she talked about how her husband didn't even know what brand of toilet paper he used every day, there were mutterings of a shared experience of frustration.

"Hey, I'll bet you he knows what brand Michael Jordan uses," one woman said.

"Why should you even have to tell him?"

"Why do we always have to be the ones who have to keep explaining everything?"

"Are they really that dumb, or do they just not care?"

When Kelly said, "You've just got to deal with it, because they're not going to change, so you have to find another solution," they really did not want to hear it.

"Why do we always have to be the ones to make the adjustment?"

"Why do we always have to be the ones to deal with it?"

"If he really respected me . . ."

"If he really loved me . . ."

I was amazed at how hard it was for these women to let go of their anger, their indignation, their frustration, and—most important—their insistence that there was only one solution to this problem.

I was amazed but not surprised. I knew the feeling, too. I've felt it as strongly as anyone. It *is* hard to accept that people who are supposed to have some kind of concern for us can't be attuned to our lives.

But I also know, by this time in my life, that it's a feeling we have to overcome.

I've heard this feeling described a hundred different ways. I know that there's a crazy satisfaction we get in seeing our worst expectations of ourselves realized. That script goes: *Yes, once again I've had it proven to me that I really don't count for enough, even from the people who are supposed to love me the most.*

On the other side of the coin, this same feeling plays into a game of one-upmanship. That game goes more or less like this: If you forget something that, according to my rules, you ought to remember, then you owe me. The name of this game is *Gotcha!* and it's not necessarily a dangerous game, although any game that turns a relationship into a contest is not the healthiest game in the world. However, women and men have probably been playing this one since Paleolithic days ("Woolly mammoth? How many times do I have to tell you that when the moon rises straight above the mountain, I always serve saber-toothed tiger? If you really loved me, you'd remember that"), and we've survived as a species.

But dangerous or not, it isn't the best way of gaining peace of mind, and it certainly isn't the most efficient way of running a household.

A High-Stakes Game

Gotcha! is a game you would never play at the office—the stakes are too high.

But the stakes are plenty high at home, too. There's your sanity, for a start. And quality time with your family. And the example you're setting for your kids.

The difference in the office is not that the stakes are higher. It's that they're more measurable. Jobs have to be done on a deadline because if they aren't, sales will be lost, contracts will be voided, competitors will steal your business.

That objective measure gives you a more specific focus. Those deadlines—those ledgers, those sales, those very tangible things—create structure. But the principle is still the same—*what do you most want to accomplish?* If what you most want to accomplish is getting the task completed, then you need to take the steps—*steps that you actually know how to take, steps that you have taken in the context of your job*—necessary to get the task completed.

We have a tendency to go on automatic pilot at home, in a way we never would at the office. We assume that things are going to get done because we've thought about them—and if we can think about them, why can't everyone? And when they don't, it drives us crazy.

The solution is simple. If you want your eleven-year-old to take a shower before you go to Grandma's, tell him.

Project Manager: Jill Staines, twenty-eight, runs own catering supplies business. Single mom of Janna, six.

I actually tried this one time at my office, just as an experiment. I couldn't have done it if we weren't a very close-knit group and if we hadn't all known in advance that it was just an experiment—and even so, we all ended up nearly killing each other.

(First, I should point out that I'm not a total idiot—I had backup for all of these jobs so that everything got done just as it would have on a normal day.)

We designated two people in my office to be the Official *Gotcha!* Geeks. So as to be Equal Opportunity Destroyers, we chose a male and a female. I got to be the female, and Stan, one of my chief assistants, was the male.

My first task of the day was a conference call with a supplier and a client. At 9:45 I called my secretary in and asked her what had happened to my conference call.

"What call?" she asked.

"The conference call with Reynolds and Weissman."

"Excuse me, Jill, but you didn't tell me to set up a call with Mr. Reynolds and Ms. Weissman."

"What are you talking about? I told you yesterday that I'd need to work some things out with both of them. How do you think I'm going to work them out unless I talk to them on the phone? Do you think they're going to read my mind by mental telepathy?"

"I'll get them on the phone right now, Jill."

"Sure, right now. It's probably too late already."

(Bill Reynolds and Janet Weissman are old poker-playing pals of mine, and were in on the experiment.)

When Cyndy got them on the phone, I started the conversation off with my office door open, so she could hear me: "Hello, Bill, Janet? I hope it's not too late. Yes, I know it was a rush job, but my secretary *somehow forgot* to set up the call this morning . . ."

People told me afterward that Cyndy was gritting her teeth, and her knuckles were white from digging her fingers into her palms—and this was in spite of the fact that she *knew* it was all play-acting.

Stan, meanwhile, was even worse than I was—because he didn't warn his "victim" in advance. He confronted a driver who'd just come to check in after completing a delivery.

"You know, there was another job you could have picked up while you were out," he told the driver.

"You should have called me," she said.

"Well, I would have thought that you would have had enough consideration to have called in from the road to see if there was anything else you could do."

"Hey, man, I didn't know . . ."

Stan put on his most forlorn, hangdog face. "No, it's all right. You cost the company a valuable order, and I guess I'll have to answer to Jill for it. I just wish people would show a little more consideration around here."

"Hey, look, I'm sorry, Stan," said the bewildered driver. "But . . ."

It actually didn't get any farther than that. Stan was all set to carry it on, but the guy at the next desk started howling with laughter.

We didn't manage to keep the act up past lunchtime. But by then, we calculated, we would have lost one regular customer, at least $5,000 in orders, and two or three good employees.

Thank goodness the only thing we really lost was the cost of taking Cyndy and a few other people we'd driven half crazy out to dinner to make amends for our behavior.

It makes a good story to tell, but it wasn't fun at all when we were doing it, because I kept telling myself: This is crazy. You're acting completely nuts.

And it's funny. I *have* acted that way at home, and I never thought I was acting crazy.

Now, I know what some of you are saying. You actually have had bosses like this. So have I. They were all people who cost their company money, and who cost their company good employees, because anyone who worked for them, and who had any creativity or sensitivity, immediately started looking for a transfer to a new department or left the company altogether. Yes, there are horrible examples in the business world—probably worse than anything we could find at home. Needless to say, these aren't the role models we'll be choosing.

Project Manager: Cassandra Warren, thirty-one, human resources manager. Married, mom of James, eleven.

One of the insidious things about *Gotcha!* is that you really don't know you're doing it. I was sure *I* wasn't doing it. I decided to try giving detailed instructions, even written instructions, to my family on what I needed them to do, but I didn't really feel like I was solving a problem. I felt like a fool.

At the same time, I realized that I did all those things as a matter of course at work. If I had a phone conversation, I followed it up with a memo. If I needed something done, I sent a written memo. If I was satisfied with what my staff did, or if I thought they could have done better, I let them know with a memo. I left a paper trail for everything I did. I would have felt like a fool if I hadn't.

When I realized that, I really started to think about this. Why would I feel like a fool at home, doing the exact same thing that made me feel like I was doing a good job at the office?

You know, you study role models a lot more consciously in the workplace than you do at home. You look at this one and that one, and you evaluate techniques that work and don't work, and you say, "I can do that," or "I would never do that," and by the time you get into a position of responsibility you've thought through a whole lot, and you've modeled yourself as the kind of boss you want to be.

You just kind of fall into the kind of mom you are, and the kind of wife you are. I know I'm a lot like my mom, and I'm proud of that, but she really doesn't have to be my only model.

What Cassandra says is true—your own mother doesn't have to be your only model. But it's a lot harder to look to different role models as a mom than as a boss.

The average American changes careers seven times during the course of a working life, and will probably have more than one boss in each company. So you'll have a veritable information bank of role models. But even in today's blended families, you'll probably have far fewer mothers than employers.

I realized just how much kids take it for granted that every household's way of doing things is like theirs when my son Rhett was three, and he went for his first play date at a friend's house.

When he came home, he said, "Mommy, that was such a weird house!"

More than a little terrified (I had been nervous enough letting him go to someone else's house alone), I asked, trying not to let my visions of everything from the Addams Family to the Mayflower Madam show through, "Really, darling? What was weird about it?"

"They didn't have any carousel animals anywhere! I looked in every room, and I couldn't find them."

You guessed it. It's Rhett's weird mom who collects antique wooden carousel animals and has them all over the house.

How do you find other role models for momhood? Look

close to you. Don't ignore your mother-in-law. Sure, she might have ways of doing things that drive you nuts, but that doesn't mean they're all bad; they might just not be what you're used to. Talk to your women friends. The first stories are always going to be the funny/horror stories about the weird things their mothers did (and still do), but there'll be other stories, too, of problem-solving skills and ways of looking at family situations that you never thought of.

There aren't any mothers, or mothers-in-law, in a corporation. But there are boards of directors, and there are outside consultants, that even CEOs can turn to. "When I want your opinion, I'll tell you what it is" is the ideal reply of our fantasies, but in real life, diplomacy is the key to good management, and it's a skill for which every one of us, in business or at home, can always use a refresher course. Once we accept that we don't live in a vacuum, we can open ourselves up to a variety of possibilities. An advisory board of experts and distinguished people in the field can be a help to any business.

When I have a problem with my kids, or any other household problem, I call my own "advisory board." I call my mother, even though I'm not always going to agree with her advice. I call my grandmother, who always has her own perspective on things, and my two sisters, who have a whole different perspective on my mother as a role model. I call a few best friends. I'm guaranteed to get different opinions from everyone I call.

I can't possibly follow all of them. But I can learn from all of them.

Does It Matter Profoundly?

At my sister's wedding, the rabbi gave her and her husband this piece of advice for getting through the hard times in a marriage: "If one of you is starting to get upset about something the other one has done," he said, "take the time to stop and ask yourself, 'Does it matter profoundly?' If it doesn't, why are you getting so upset?"

Ever since then, I've tried to make sure that I classify my annoyances, grievances, and outrages into one of two categories: this doesn't really matter profoundly, or this is truly *not* okay.

That your spouse doesn't remember what kind of toilet paper you use really doesn't matter profoundly. It's not the sort of thing you have to fight over. What you win is real, but it isn't worth winning, and what you lose is a lot more significant.

Project Manager: Diane DeRhome, thirty-nine, graphic designer. Remarried, mom by previous marriage of Sabine, thirteen, and Deborah, nine.

I saw a therapist for a short time a few years ago, and one insight I got from therapy has really stayed with me. I said something offhand to my therapist along the lines of, "Oh, you know, my usual fear of rejection." She said, "I don't think you have a fear of rejection."

"What do you mean?" I asked defensively. I was very possessive about my fear of rejection in those days.

"Why should you have a fear of rejection?" she asked. "You know what rejection is like. You've experienced it often enough. You know when it's coming, you know what it feels like, you know how to handle it, you know what to do next."

"So what would you call it?" I asked.

"How about fear of acceptance?" she said. "Now, there's a frightening concept. There's something you're not used to, something you don't know how you'd handle. *That's* the unknown."

I thought about it, and it made sense. Gradually, I started looking at myself in relationships and finding the courage to take chances with men who might actually accept me. It seems to have worked—I'm happily married now, and have been for five years.

Eventually—and it certainly was not right away—I was able to build on that insight and come to understand what *Gotcha!* meant to me.

I had always thought that when my husband let me down, it was a little defeat for me—but what the heck, I was used to losing. Suddenly it occurred to me that to understand my own behavior, I should do the same thing that therapist had done—stand my preconceptions on their head and look at them from the other end.

Did I really want *that* victory? Was it as good as the other possible victory, which would be to get to the theater on time, to make sure the check really got mailed to the credit card company before we owed a penalty on it, to have the right kind of wine for the dinner I'd planned? And to know that all this had come about because I had seen to it?

I realized . . . I didn't know. I had no experience with that sort of victory.

So there it was again: fear of the unknown. That's when I vowed to work on never setting up a *Gotcha!* again.

Anti-Gotcha! *Tactics*

Gotcha! isn't going to go away until you develop a workable tactic for ending it.

A family strategy session is a good place to begin, so call a family meeting.

I'll discuss family meetings at greater length in another chapter, but let me just put in a few words here about family meetings as they relate to anti-*Gotcha!* tactics.

If the family, with you as CEO, is sometimes employees, sometimes board of directors, they're very definitely the latter in a family meeting. Everyone should have input at these "board of directors' meetings," and everyone's input should be respected.

But here's a rule that every good parliamentarian knows.

She who controls the agenda controls the meeting.

Here's the agenda you'll want to bring to this meeting.

▶ **Make a list** of all the *Gotcha!*s that everyone in the house is aware of. Make sure that everyone in the family participates in this exercise.

   Start it yourself, to get the ball rolling, with some *Gotcha!*s that you know you're guilty of.

   Make it clear, however, that this is not a *mea culpa* session, where people are simply supposed to come clean with their own failings. You want to make a list of everything that everyone in the house sees as a *Gotcha!* mechanism.

   No one is allowed, during this phase, to comment or act defensive.

   Write everything down.

▶ **Discuss how to solve the problem.** Keep all discussion focused on this issue—not whose fault it is, but how to solve the problem. Give your family this message: *It has to work.* It doesn't matter how we get there. There are all sorts of ways to solve any problem, and we'll find the best one for our family. But the problem has to be solved, and we expect that it will be solved.

The most familiar *Gotcha!* scenario is something that doesn't get done, although you can't imagine how anyone could not know that you expect it to be done. For example— you expect the kids to clean up the family room every night before they go to bed. If you stand over them and tell them to do it every night, you'll feel like a nag and they'll tell you you're a nag. Besides, it means you have to go down to the family room every night and tell them—and if they're teenagers, there's a good chance you'll be going to bed before they do. On the other hand, if you don't tell them every night, they won't do it.

What's the solution? Ask them to come up with one. Make it clear, however, that you need this problem solved. Let them figure out the best way for them to receive information. Would a written reminder on the door of their rooms work? Would a penalty be appropriate, like not allowing them to use the family room for a period of time?

When my kids were little, I had a "Saturday box" for toys that weren't picked up. Anything that was left in the family room at the end of the day was picked up, put in the box, and they didn't get it back until Saturday. It worked. The kids seemed to think it was fair. They felt, since they realized they had control over the situation, that it was their solution as much as it was mine. It felt like a team effort. It also, over a relatively short period of time, did the job. The kids started picking up their toys.

Gotcha! *and Process vs. Project*

A solution-oriented approach is, ultimately, the answer to *Gotcha!* The solution is a project; *Gotcha!* is a process, never-ending and self-defeating. Like most processes, it creates an endless amount of busywork without ever leading anywhere. Like all too many household processes, it creates the illusion that you *can't* solve the problem.

It's wise, here, to go back to your workplace experience for a lesson. In the workplace, we *expect* things to work. We set up a project with the expectation that it will

work, and we analyze it afterward. If the project is successful, we can build on it and use it as a model for future projects. If it's not, we analyze why not and we modify our
strategies.

Sometimes, just making yourself clearer goes a long way
toward arriving at a solution. If your husband offers to do
some of the shopping for you, he's probably doing it to help.

Being a Good Boss

When you get right down to it, the whole *Gotcha!* situation is
directly related to the question of what makes a good boss.
Here's what I mean. The following is a short list of the basic
qualities of being a good boss:

▶ **Don't abdicate your decision making role.**
You're running the organization because you're the
one who's best qualified. You're the one who has
created the mission statement. So while you don't
want to get nuts over something that does not matter
profoundly—like when you send your husband out
to get olive oil and balsamic vinegar, and he comes
home with Crispy-Raspberry Dressing—you do want
to remind him that you're running an organization,
and there is a master plan at work here . . . and that
"Honey, can I help?" is a *contractual obligation*.

▶ **Make sure you have the high ground.** *Gotcha!* is a
game that everyone plays, and your goal is to identify it and eliminate it from *everybody's* arsenal. Your
authority to do this becomes strongest when you
start with yourself first.

▶ **Communicate your expectations.** This is, of
course, the heart of the *Gotcha!* strategy, but it's re-

ally the heart of all management strategy. Don't
make people guess what you want.

▶ **Don't set someone up to fail.** The truth is, this
does happen at work. You might do it if you want
to get rid of someone, although it's not a very good
technique. But at home? This is your family. No
downsizing, remember? So there is *no* good reason
to set someone up to fail, except to satisfy a need
that is best left unsatisfied. And this need will go
away by itself when your household starts running
better.

▶ **Create job descriptions.** This means job descriptions for your kids, and also job descriptions for you
and your partner. What does "clean your room"
mean? How is it different from "clean the house" or
"clean the kitchen"? You know what the difference
is; have you articulated it to everyone involved?

Let's say you have an agreement with your
husband that he fixes dinner for the kids twice a
week. Do you and he have the same definition of
"dinner"? You won't know unless "fixing dinner" is
explained in detail.

When we start talking about job descriptions,
we're not just talking about family job descriptions,
either. What about job descriptions for a nanny, or a
housekeeper, or someone who comes in to clean
once a week? Are you as clear with these people as
you are with the people who report to you at work?
Finally, don't forget that your kids' job descriptions
will be constantly changing as they get older and
more capable of taking responsibility or working independently. You'll have to articulate that new responsibility to them and make sure they understand
that "yard work" does not have the same job description for a fourteen-year-old that it has for a
nine-year-old.

Those job descriptions will change once again as your kids get still older and start taking on more responsibilities outside the home.

Don't forget one major difference between work and home. You're training your employees at work to stay with the company, to advance and become more productive members of your workforce. You're training your staff at home to leave the company.

Chapter 7

You Can't Fire Your Family

Most people never fire anyone. There's an image of the typical CEO as someone like "Chainsaw Al" Dexter, the infamous boss of several different corporations in the Nineties, who would come in, take over a company, and slash 25 percent of its workforce. But even "Chainsaw Al" didn't call each one of those five or ten thousand workers in, look each one in the eye, and say "Sam, you're fired."

Alison has had to fire a few people during the course of her career, and it's been gut-wrenching each time. This week, she fired a secretary who was chronically late, had a hostile attitude, and might have been dishonest. She had never seemed as if she gave a damn, and Alison fully expected her to fly into a rage, level a few choice obscenities at Alison, and storm out.

Instead, she broke down in tears. She told Alison, between sobs, of the stress she'd been under at home, the migraines she'd been having. She told Alison how much she needed the job, how desperate her financial situation was. She told Alison how much she admired her and what an inspiration it had been to work in a department where she was the boss.

It was all too late to make any difference; the decision had been made. Alison had to go ahead and fire the woman.

She didn't get a lot done for the rest of the day. She took care of things that absolutely had to be taken care of, and she left work right at five.

She sat alone at a diner for about half an hour, nursing a cup of coffee and a refill. She didn't want anything except to be alone for a while. When she left, she gave the waitress a generous tip for taking up her time, and perhaps as a reparation to all women who are eking out a living on tough, subsistence-level jobs. She drove home slowly.

As it happened, Whitney was in a teenage mood on that same afternoon. It doesn't matter what the problem was. She started with Alison; Alison didn't give the right answers, whatever they were; Whitney exploded; Alison snapped back; Whitney called her a tyrant and stormed out, slamming the door behind her.

Later that evening, Alison was on the phone with a friend, who asked her during the course of the conversation how things were going with Whitney. Alison told her. "Well," the friend said philosophically, "too bad you can't fire your relatives."

Alison didn't stay on the phone much longer. It wasn't her friend's fault that she'd pressed that particular button, but Alison just didn't feel like talking anymore.

Can't fire your relatives, she thought. Who would want to? Who would want to fire anybody?

But as she spent a quiet evening by herself (making lunches; it relaxed her and helped her do some of her best thinking), her mind started turning to the office. You can't fire your relatives. Well, there are lots of other people you can't fire, either. You can't fire your bosses. You can't fire people who work in departments that don't report to you. You can't fire your customers, or people who work for your associates. You can't fire union shop stewards or civil ser-

*vants and government officials you have to deal with for
permits or OSHA requirements. And those are just people
you might want to fire. What about partners, close associates, valued subordinates who are, for one reason or another, giving you huge short-term problems or aggravation?*

What are the management tools we use in the office for
dealing with difficult personal problems? How do we handle
the people we can't—or don't want to—fire?

Here are two rules of thumb we use at the office and
that we can adapt for use at home:

1. Be consistent.
2. Be flexible.

How is that possible? Simple. Each of these rules is applied somewhat differently. You want to be consistent in de-
lineating your goals and keeping your eyes on them. This
means that you need a *vision*.

You want to be flexible in dealing with individuals, in
order to direct them to those consistent goals. This means
that you need to understand that ultimately it's realizing the
vision that is important. You don't have to be wedded to the
idea that there's only one way to reach that vision.

The first thing any manager needs to learn is that being a
manager is not a popularity contest. Whether people like you
or not is nowhere near as important as what has to be accomplished.

It's easy to see this in action at the office. If you're
working against a deadline—if the mechanicals for those new
brochures have to be at the printer's by ten A.M. Thursday—
it becomes manifestly clear that who likes you or doesn't like
you shrinks to a very tiny measure of importance in comparison to the importance of making the deadline.

What's at stake at home is so much greater: our children's safety, security, and happiness. And while we know that being a mother isn't a popularity contest, we are also very much aware that what our children think of us does matter. It matters deeply.

In the office, we're focused on the job, the product, the end result. The people we work with, no matter how much we like them, are a means to that end. At home, the people *are* the end product. Nevertheless, the principles of personnel management are still relevant.

In the office, the basic tenet of communication is to recognize that people are different and that to get the best out of them you have to understand their differences.

Former major league baseball manager Billy Martin used to say, "A baseball team is made of twenty-five individuals. At any given time, five of them will like you, five of them will hate you, and the rest won't have made up their minds yet. Your job is to keep the five who hate you away from the ones who haven't made up their minds."

With the ones who like you (admire you, see you as a role model), you'll work creatively. You'll try new things, you'll give them the opportunity to work more independently, and you'll go to them with those off-the-wall ideas that can lead to breakthroughs if they really work out.

With the ones who might like you, but are not yet firmly in your camp, you'll be more nurturing. You'll bring them along more slowly. You'll understand that you can't go into a project assuming that they'll want to follow your suggestions just because they're yours, so you'll have to prove yourself to them. You'll understand, as well, that they won't be so closely attuned to your way of approaching a problem that you can count on them to work with minimal supervision. You'll have to work more closely with them and review their work more often.

With the ones who don't much like you, you can try to

be nurturing to win them over, but you have to accept that there's every chance you won't succeed. Presumably, these people are on your team because of their skills. Take advantage of those skills. Use them, but know that you're not going to be able to expect much more from them than performance of that limited specialty. On the job, you'll have to understand even more about the psyche of your recalcitrant specialist. Should you monitor her work carefully or give her a wide berth and leave her alone? If pride in her specialty means more to her than her aversion to you, then leaving her alone is probably the best plan.

You might also, in dealing with an employee who doesn't much like you, depersonalize the situation by putting everything in terms of the corporate vision.

Certainly, not every business is run this way. Many bosses are obstinate, egocentric, short-tempered martinets with no people skills at all. Some of them are successful. Maybe they have an incredibly creative vision. Maybe they're just ruthless, and they can keep going as long as they can find enough employees who are willing to be bullied so that they can get the job done.

We know about bosses like this. We'd rather not work for them, as a general rule, and they aren't the bosses we choose as role models.

By the same token, there are strange, unconventional parents who seem to break every rule of management, who seem to be blissfully unaware of any needs other than their own. Some of them have kids who survive and even thrive, and who might grow up to write frightening but affectionate memoirs like Patrick Dennis's *Auntie Mame* or Carrie Fisher's *Postcards from the Edge*. But these aren't the role models we want to choose for our own parenting archetypes, either.

Gotcha! *and Family Personnel Management*

When we think about using managerial skills with a difficult family member, we have to take into account the *Gotcha!* temptation. It's the easiest thing in the world to turn kids into self-fulfilling prophecies—"Oh, it's the terrible twos" or "He's just acting like a typical teenager."

This is easy to fall into, because there really are terrible twos, and there really is typical teenage behavior. If you want to take the attitude that things are beyond your control, you can always find justification. It will always be very good, solid justification, too. But the end result will be that things remain out of your control.

If you find yourself saying "See what I mean? That's how she always is!" about a child, chances are you aren't paying enough attention to the full range of personnel management tools available to you.

The tools are there. So is your experience, and your experience will tell you that these are problems that can be solved, one way or another. Sometimes your child is going to be one of those employees who don't like you. When you're dealing with your own children, it's hard to remember that this is not the end of the world. But it's not.

Nobody is going to hate you forever. If it's someone you work with—a fellow employee, customer, or co-contractor— he'll eventually either come around and learn to like you or he'll move on. A child won't move on, but he will eventually come around.

Or he will move on, in a way. As I said before, when you're discussing a family as a management unit, you're talking about an organization with an incredible turnover of personnel.

And, since a family is its own most important commodity, that five-year-old, that eleven-year-old, that fourteen-year-old who comes along next year is going to be the newest member of your project team—but also the finished product of your old team.

So don't worry too much about not always being the most popular mom on the block. It's a necessary part of any management strategy. "You don't have to like me," my mother would tell me when we were at loggerheads, "but you have to respect me."

I grew up to love her, like her, *and* respect her.

Family Management and Discipline: Peg and Alison

It's time for Peg and Mike to have a serious talk. It's an old story—who's responsible for disciplining the kids? Peg grew up hearing "Wait till your father gets home," and she drifted into saying it herself with her own family. (Although these days, with Mike working second shift, it's "Wait till your father wakes up.")

"I'm sick of it," Mike tells her. "Do you think I want my kids getting scared of me as soon as I walk in the door?"

"I don't see why you have to worry about that," Peg says. "It's not as though you ever do anything. They could set your shoes on fire while you were wearing them, and you wouldn't notice unless the smoke blocked your view of the TV."

One of the things that keeps Peg's and Mike's marriage on an even keel, and keeps their arguments from escalating into full-fledged fights, is that Peg can always crack Mike up.

But at this point, it's clear that they're going nowhere.

Peg realizes that they've fallen into one of the classic models of the home/process vs. work/project. They go on repeating a pattern that makes neither of them happy and doesn't solve the problem, just because it's how they've always done it.

They go back to square one. First they define the problem: discipline in their family is not organized or consistent, and no one really knows who's responsible for what.

The allocation of personnel is easy: Peg and Mike. It is absolutely clear that this is a project for only the two of them. They're not going to ask for input from the kids.

They need to create a strategy in two parts. First, they need to agree on an appropriate discipline for a variety of everyday situations, which will give them a framework for addressing specific problems as they come up.

Second, they need to figure out how to share the responsibility. Obviously, Peg doesn't want to be the only one who ends up having to take on the role of disciplinarian, and since she's the one who is on the scene more often, she's the one who's generally on the front line.

They agree that discipline has to be administered in direct response to the behavior. But they also agree that there are two kinds of issues: the immediate problems that get dealt with right away, and the ones that repeat over and over. They agree that for any repeating problem, the parent who hasn't been the first line of discipline will become the second line. The parent will sit down with the child, make it absolutely clear that both parents are together on this, and institute whatever steps are appropriate. This second line of discipline will not be put off or avoided, and it can be called in by the first parent whenever she/he thinks it's necessary.

Finally—and here's the key—Peg and Mike agree that they'll sit down again in a month, and again in three months, to review the project.

What if you *have* fired part of your family? What if you're divorced? Does that make things easier?

Not hardly. Alison's problem with discipline-as-popularity-contest is much tougher than Peg's.

Alison's ex seems to think that family management is a matter of who scores the most personality points. He and his trophy wife, since they got together (well, since they got together officially, which was when he left Alison for her), made a point of turning weekend visits into a kind of Disney World meets Ben and Jerry, including advice about handling Mom's rules that consisted of "You know how your mother is" delivered with a conspiratorial chuckle.

There's nothing harder on a family than that kind of pressure. You can't treat your ex as a business competitor, even if he's treating you that way. You can't engage in a price war or an advertising war.

Was there any way that Alison could bring her workplace skills to bear on this one? At first, she wasn't sure she saw a way.

The Work-to-Home Translator

This is a device that can prove worthwhile as a brainstorming tool for bringing work solutions home, and it's one that Alison used in this situation.

Start by making up a chart with four boxes in it, labeled like this:

1. What is this problem? How do I define it?
2. How have I handled this problem/seen this problem handled at work?
3. How is my home situation different?
4. How do I adapt the work solution to home?

Be creative when you take out your work-to-home translator. You're looking for solutions to difficult problems, and they aren't always going to be in the first place you look.

Some theorists divide our thinking functions into *left-brain activity* and *right-brain activity*. According to them, the two hemispheres of the human brain perform different functions. The left brain is logical, analytical. It likes to break things down into component parts. The right brain is intuitive, mystical, holistic, creative.

At first glance, the work-to-home translator looks like a left-brain creation. It calls upon you to analyze, to compare, to break things into components. But it won't work for you unless you allow yourself to use your right brain, the side of your brain that's open to unexpected, intuitive leaps, too. Alison would never have come up with the solution she did arrive at if she hadn't been able to make that leap, to see that "everyone has a place" meant something completely different at work than it did at home.

When you set up a work-to-home translator, make those boxes big ones. Take a whole piece of paper, and divide it into quarters. Then just start writing things down. Don't think, don't censor, don't edit yourself. Leave yourself open to those ideas you didn't know you had.

Here are some of Alison's exercises with the work-to-home translator:

What is this problem? How do I define it?

Discipline . . .

Two messages . . . conflicting messages

Torn between two values—what's the difference between them?

How have I handled this problem/seen this problem handled at work?

Two competing companies?—No—two companies with one employer? That doesn't work.

So . . . one company, two bosses? That's more like it . . . two divisions, employee torn between them.

As employee—I've been there, done that, won't do it again.

How did I get out from under it?

No way around it—just finally had to declare myself out—which wasn't easy.

As boss? You finally have to stop focusing on what a jerk the other guy is and bring your focus back to the company.

How is my home situation different?

It's not two divisions of the same company—we don't report to the same overall boss, we don't have the same overall goals. How can you arrive at any sort of meeting of the minds like this?

How do I adapt the work solution to home?

Have to take it on myself . . . have to articulate a vision that I can communicate to both ex-husband and kids.

Talk to kids about how I handled similar situations.

Alison sat down with her kids and told them that if there were any problems between her and her husband's new wife, they weren't the kids' problems and that the kids didn't have to be in the middle of them.

This was not an easy sell. Kids don't like being told that they're just kids and that they're too young to understand, even if you don't think that's what you're saying. They don't like to feel as if they're being left out.

Alison talked to them about her own worst experience at work, being caught between two feuding bosses. "I was still in college, and I was working my way through by managing a restaurant that was owned by a married couple who were heading for divorce. They really hated each other, and each of them took me aside and let me know all this awful stuff about the other that I didn't want to know. Then they stopped talking to each other altogether, and they just communicated through me. I hated it, but I didn't dare say anything because I really needed the job."

"What happened?" Trevor asked.

"They fired me," Alison told him. "After a while, they'd both told me so many ugly stories about the other that neither of them trusted me. So some years later, when I was out of college and working, I ran into the same situation. At first I tried to handle it the same way, just by keeping my mouth shut, but then I remembered how much good that had done me the last time, and I told them I absolutely refused to get in the middle. It was scary, but it worked. Before I took that stand, I was afraid that if I didn't know everything that was going on, I'd lose control of the situation. But I realized that I didn't have any control of the situation, and by being forceful I had taken control of myself."

Do your kids listen to you? Sometimes they do. A few weeks later, the kids were spending the weekend with their father. When the stepmother started to say something snide about Alison, Trevor walked over to the phone and dialed Alison's number. Then he handed the phone to his stepmother. "Here," he said. "Why don't you tell Mom this? I think this is between you and her."

It was a start. Alison had solved a major problem, but there were others.

For Alison, the problems with her ex came to a head last year, when Whitney announced that her mother was a tyrant and didn't understand her and she wanted to go live with her father.

First, Alison followed my basic rule for dealing with

corporate adversity: Don't ever let them see you cry. Alison has cried in front of her kids. She's shared her emotions with them. But as much as this hurt her, she knew that it was Whitney's crisis, not hers.

"Are you sure that's what you want?" she asked.

She could see a flicker of doubt in Whitney's eyes.

"Yes, I'm sure," Whitney said.

"Have you talked to your father about it?"

"No, but I know he'll want me. He really loves me."

Alison wasn't so sure. She made the first phone call, and she could hear the all-too-familiar sound of her ex trying to disguise rising panic at the prospect of having to take responsibility. But he brazened his way through it, and by the time he spoke to Whitney, he was SuperDad.

Alison took on a new project—the management of Whitney's living-with-Dad experiment.

She had tea after school with Whitney every Wednesday and kept her weekends open for Whitney to come visit—if Whitney let her know by Wednesday that she wanted to come.

It was the third Wednesday when she started to hear a crack in Whitney's optimism, and it was two weeks later that Whitney said, for the first time, "I want to come home."

It was the other side of the ex's view of parenthood as competition. Now Whitney's dad had decided that he was going to prove what an unsuccessful parent Alison had been. Whitney was underachieving at school? (She was, but it wasn't serious; Alison was working on solving it.) Well, he was going to show how a parent could produce straight A's. Whitney was getting too serious about her boyfriend? (She wasn't.) Well, he was going to show how a real parent protected his daughter from no-good teenage boys. He was going to protect her from other girls who were a bad influence on her, too—no trips to the mall unless the stepmother was with her at all times.

"I feel like I'm in prison, Mom," Whitney said. "Can't I come home?"

"You have to finish the semester at school," Alison told her. "You've started there; you have to see it through."

"Can I come and stay with you on weekends?"

"Of course you can, dear."

"And can I see Scott on weekends?"

"I won't do anything behind your father's back," Alison told her. "But I'll talk to him."

She had an idea what the conversation would be like, except it was worse than she had expected it to be. He was taking her to court, he was going to prove that she was an unfit mother for endangering her daughter's morals, he would see that she only had supervised visitation.

He never did take her to court. Whitney moved back to her old room in June and registered for school in Alison's hometown for the fall. She spent a lot of time on the phone with her friends, discussing (among other things) what courses they'd be taking, what teachers they'd have. She broke up with Scott. After that she saw Steve—until she broke up with him. She told Alison she was looking forward to spending the summer free, without some dumb boy hanging around.

After the emotional storms had subsided, Alison realized that something had to be done. She and Whitney's father had to have more of an agreement on discipline issues.

Alison went back to her work-to-home translator. Was there any connection between her and the ex that could possibly relate to her business world experience? He wasn't a rival company. But he wasn't part of the same company, either. They had no common boss that they could go to ask for mediation.

No common boss, perhaps . . . but didn't they have a common mission?

You need to be flexible in dealing with individuals, she remembered. You need to understand that ultimately it's important to realize the shared vision. You don't have to be wedded to the idea that there's only one way to reach that vision.

Of course she and her ex had a common vision, Alison realized: to raise healthy, happy, responsible children.

Any fruitful discussion had to focus on the vision, not on recriminations and countercharges about who had done what or who was at fault on this, that, or the other thing.

Back to the Future

Visualization is a technique that is recommended by motivational psychologists and management strategists alike as one of the best ways to successfully achieve goals. In visioning, instead of thinking of something you'd like to achieve and then wondering how the heck you're going to do it, you start by imagining yourself as *having done it already,* and then you go back and figure out how you did it.

In my earlier book, *Making Change,* I introduced a visioning technique I use in my seminars and that I call *Back to the Future.*

It works like this:

- ▶ Decide where you want to be.
- ▶ Picture yourself there.
- ▶ Now work five steps backward in time and see how it is that you got there, step by step.

If you're imagining a promotion to vice president, picture yourself in the office, as vividly as you can. What does the decor look like? What's the view from the window? What's in your in box? With whom do you have appointments that morning?

If you want to write a book, imagine the book written and published. Imagine yourself in the biggest bookstore in New York City, signing autographs. What does the dust jacket look like? What do the reviews say?

Then do the same thing as you work backward in time, counting each step down as though you were counting off a space launching from Cape Canaveral. For each step, picture yourself *there*. When you get to the last step, it's time to *Blast off!*

When you have those five steps vividly re-created in your mind, reverse them so that they're going forward in time, and there's your plan of action.

Here's how Alison made up her *Back to the Future:*

Back to the Future: My ex and I have agreed on a plan for communicating about discipline for the kids.

5. We're having lunch together at a neutral site, and each of us is contributing positive ideas about what the kids need in the way of discipline. If we start feeling the need to criticize the other, we go back to our shared mission statement and get back on track.

4. We've agreed to meet and discuss discipline face-to-face, both abiding by a shared vision and ground rules for discussion.

3. Before we even discuss actually meeting, we've agreed in principle on a shared mission statement: to raise happy, responsible, and productive children.

2. In a series of E-mails, we've created a shared mission statement. I've taken the lead here, keeping the discussion focused on what's best for the kids and not getting into being defensive about his criticisms or making criticisms of him. That's why I've chosen E-mail for this dialogue—I can count to ten every time I start to get mad.

1. I'm taking the first step. I'm sending him an E-mail initiating the discussion.

.... *Blast Off!*. . . . . . .

Negotiation and Intervention

Management is a constant game of adjustment. You need to know when it's a good idea to negotiate and when it isn't. This is based on a couple of factors: whether there's room for compromise, and how your employee/associate will respond to your suggestions. It's the same with kids.

I've talked about how to deal with employees or associates who don't get along with you. What about dealing with employees or associates who don't get along with each other? This might be a problem at work; it's virtually a way of life at home. Conflict resolution is one of the most important management skills you can master.

When I have two employees who don't get along with each other, the first question I ask myself is: Should I intervene?

When in doubt, the answer probably is no. For one thing, it's no fun to get involved in a dispute between two other people. For another, the solutions that people arrive at on their own are often the best solutions. However, the fact that an intervention *is* unpleasant can tempt you to hold back longer than you should. I always made it a point to keep a close eye on a developing situation.

If I decided to intervene—or if both of the employees came to me—I'd always start by talking to each one of them separately, because when you start talking to both of them together you are outnumbered by two people who have more in common than they think. They actually agree with each other, and disagree with you, on the question of what the most important issue is.

They think the most important issue is whatever it is that they're fighting over. *You* know that it's really getting the organization back on an even track and getting on with what's really important. When you have them separated, you can bypass their issue and go straight to yours.

This is as true for kids as it is for employees. With little kids, you can just tell them to take a time-out, and pretty soon their desire to play with each other will overcome their grievance.

You can't be sure that this will be the case with older kids, for whom disagreements can be more substantive and problems can fester. So the first management skill you need is sensitivity to the situation. You have to know when to step in before things get out of hand.

First, as with employees, talk to each child separately. Start by setting the terms of the discussion. Make it clear from the outset that we're not going to be discussing whose fault it was that both of them were grounded. We're going to talk about the family and how to get it working together.

Ask for your child's ideas, then let him talk. Let him introduce ideas and run with them—but they'll be ideas about how to advance your agenda. Do the same with the other feuding child. When you finally bring the two of them together, the agenda will be clear: how to get past their differences and work together.

When I've used this approach at work, sometimes it's been so successful that the two individuals ended up having a stronger bond with each other than either of them had with me. That was okay with me—as long as it was good for the company. It's certainly okay at home.

Giving Yourself Space

Managing a company can be a high-pressure job, but parenting can be too.

Giving your kids a time-out is an effective parenting technique that we've all used; it can defuse a potentially difficult situation and give the child a chance to release a certain amount of stress. Don't forget that the same technique can work for you, too.

It's true in business. There are some decisions that have to be made instantly, but more do not. A good manager knows the difference.

It's true at home, too. Children tend to think that if they want an answer or a decision, it has to be given right now, but it doesn't. This isn't a copout; it's just managerial good sense. If you're not ready to handle a problem, and it's not a matter of life or death, then "I'll take that under advisement and get back to you" is a perfectly acceptable answer—in business *or* at home.

A Family Mission Statement

When little kids get over their differences after a time-out and start playing together again, they have adopted a mission statement, and they're staying focused on it.

Their mission statement is *Play and have fun.*

This is actually a model mission statement. It's short. It's to the point. You can build on it. And if you start to lose your sense of direction, it's a good compass point to bring you back. Anything else you might add to it, like *Learn to respect other people's things,* is basically a means to that end.

Will a family mission statement help you?

I believe it will.

A family is more complex than any other organization. It is held together by the most intricate weave of emotional fabric. It is a multigenerational mélange of people who, in many ways, have very little in common, yet who have an overriding interest in getting along and maintaining a close and supportive relationship.

For all those reasons, I'd say there's no organization that needs a mission statement *more* than a family does.

What Goes Into a Family Mission Statement?

If a family is going to live by a mission statement, it has to be a statement the whole family can subscribe to. So it makes a difference who writes it, and how it gets written, and what goes into the writing of it.

Who writes corporate mission statements? Most of the time, no one quite knows, as near as I can make out. And if no one quite knows who wrote something, that generally means one of two things: either the boss wrote it himself but doesn't want to take responsibility for it, or it was written by committee.

We have to do better than that.

Who contributes to your mission statement depends on when you get around to writing it. I decided to make one for my family when I was divorced and bringing up two kids as a single mom. Kyle was three and Rhett was just born, so the responsibility was basically mine. Here's what I came up with.

> **To make a foundation of unconditional love on which to build a framework in which my children can learn to respect themselves and others, and pursue their visions.**

If you're writing your mission statement as a newly married couple, then you and your husband will be writing it together. Make sure that you're not making it too restrictive or setting up expectations that your future family might not want to live up to.

Here are a few examples from women I've worked with:

Project Manager: Sally Freeman, twenty-four, teacher. Mom of Toby, two.

My husband, Sam, is an artist who runs a frame shop, and I paint, too, so our first draft of a family mission statement was something like this: *To create an environment where our children's talent and love of art can flourish, and in which we'll be open to new ideas and creative innovation.*

But after a little reflection, we realized that this was something that was specifically tailored for what we might have hoped for when we were twelve or thirteen. It would have given us freedom, but it might have been a terrible straitjacket—or just irrelevant—to our kids. Suppose they don't have a love of art or any interest in developing their talents in that direction? Who knows?

How do you put what you *really* want for your family in one sentence? We went through a lot of sentences like the first one. We wanted to come up with something about encouraging creativity, in ourselves and each other as well as in our children. But we knew that a family has to be more than that. Children need structure and guidance.

For a while, we started saying "Forget creativity, let's make a mission statement that says we keep Toby absolutely safe and never let him do anything dangerous." But we knew we couldn't stick to that (though it was tempting).

Besides, we do think that creativity and exploration are important, no matter how much it might scare us. We probably scared our parents, too. So this is what we ended up with: *To provide a structured and nurturing environment in which all of us can feel encouraged to express ourselves to the limits of our potential.*

We did it in one sentence. And we think we can live with it and grow with it. I made it into a needlepoint sampler, and we have it in the kitchen.

Project Manager: Sarika Moore, forty, housewife (former restaurant manager). Mom of Stephonne, sixteen; Jerry, fourteen; William, ten; and Eriq, six.

We knew when we started to write our mission statement that our family has always been held together by religion. That was the backbone of our family, so that had to be in our mission statement.

William didn't see anything wrong with *To love God*. But we decided we needed something to bring the family into it more, so we kept thinking a little longer, and we came up with this: *To love, respect, and honor each other just as God loves us.*

We made up this mission statement five years ago, when our children were young. Now they're all growing, and we've had the strains and pains that a family has. But we've always come back to that statement, and it's always set us back on track.

Chapter 9

When It's Not Important
That *You* Do It

I t's just as well not to take this CEO thing *too* seriously. Otherwise, you might find yourself spending all your time looking at household chores and saying, "Now, would a CEO do this?"

When Peg decided to take over the role of CEO of her household, she went out to her local warehouse club, bought a director's chair, and stenciled "CEO" on the back. She's taken a lot of teasing about the chair, and that's part of why she got it: as a good-natured joke, to show that she doesn't really take this CEO thing too seriously.

She keeps the chair folded in a corner of the kitchen. When she unfolds it, someone will say, "Uh-oh! Mom's getting the chair out! We're gonna be taking some orders!"

But for all the teasing, her family knows it's for real. When the chair comes out of the corner, there'll be a serious household planning session coming up.

The rest of the time, she pitches in and does what she

has to do to keep the household running. And why shouldn't she? She's got it pretty well organized.

We all know that the point of taking over the job of CEO is to give everyone in your family a useful, involved, family-oriented role. After this managerial restructuring, you might find that certain tasks that were once done automatically are now open to question.

Basically, there are three possible directions any task can go.

1. You can go on doing it yourself.
2. You can have someone else in your family do it.
3. You can farm it out to someone totally unconnected to your family. In other words, you can outsource it.

In a business you'd outsource something if :

▶ It was cost-effective.
▶ You could find someone else who specialized in this sort of work and could, therefore, do the job better than you could get it done in house.
▶ The task wasn't something that was integral to your self-concept as a company.
▶ The task wasn't one that someone in your organization could benefit from doing.

These are pretty much the same standards you'd use at home; but at home, you'll put more emphasis on the second two considerations. Your home is not a bottom-line-oriented institution; it's more of a not-for-profit.

Here are some of the ways Alison has solved her household's problems.

Transportation Management

What needs to be done?

AFTER-SCHOOL PICKUP: Alison lives in a suburb, away from reliable public transportation. There's a school bus, but cutbacks have eliminated buses home from all after-school programs. Since she wants to encourage Whitney to get involved in activities, she has to make sure she has transportation any time she does stay after school. She couldn't keep Trevor away from his sports practices if she tied him down.

REGULAR CAR MAINTENANCE: The family has one car. It's a new one, leased. It needs regular service. And of course, it needs gas and washing.

How does it get done?

AFTER-SCHOOL PICKUP: Alison does it all—when she's in town. When she's not, she makes do as best she can. She tries to line up car pools, but these plans have an uncanny habit of falling apart at the last minute, leaving Alison making frantic long-distance calls from wherever she happens to be, looking for someone who can fill in or calling a cab company.

REGULAR CAR MAINTENANCE: Alison takes the car to the dealership for regular maintenance. When she needs gas, if she's alone, she pumps it herself. When she's with Trevor, he pumps it. When she's with Whitney . . . well, it's easier to do it herself than to get into an argument with Whitney about how Lincoln freed the slaves.

Trevor washes the car, and Alison pays him for it.

What are the other options?

Alison could outsource the after-school transportation contract. She could hire someone—a friend, or someone recommended by a friend—to ferry her kids on a regular basis for those occasions when she's out of town, or even every weekday.

She could have a standing, scheduled account with a cab company to do the same thing.

She could let her kids take responsibility for making their own arrangements (this is the choice they prefer).

What are the pros and cons?

HIRING A CAB SERVICE—PRO: It's one less thing to worry about.

HIRING A CAB SERVICE—CON: Alison feels uncomfortable about it. She lives in a neighborhood where many moms work full-time, but they don't travel as much as she does, so they're usually available to pick up their kids. She's also afraid that hiring a cab would send a message to her neighbors that she's an absentee mother, not really connected to her kids' day-to-day life

Besides, the kids don't want to be picked up by a cab. That's not what the other kids do, and they don't want to be different.

HIRING A PRIVATE INDIVIDUAL—PRO: Hiring a friend, or someone recommended by a friend, doesn't seem as impersonal.

HIRING A PRIVATE INDIVIDUAL—CON: Alison is concerned that there could be insurance ramifications here. It's also not that much more reliable than the system she's using now. If the friend gets sick or has an emergency, Alison is back to square one. If you're hiring a service that's unreliable, that's no better than not hiring anyone at all.

LETTING THE KIDS HANDLE IT—PRO: If Alison is concerned with appearances, the kids, being kids, are even more concerned with appearances. Maybe it's time to start giving the kids more responsibility. This is a responsibility they're ready to take.

LETTING THE KIDS HANDLE IT—CON: Kids always seem to be ready to take on the responsibilities they're *not* ready for, and least willing to take on the responsibilities they can and should be taking, like carrying out the garbage. Alison considered this one for a New York minute before rejecting it. It's her responsibility. End of story.

What's the choice?

AFTER-SCHOOL PICKUP: Alison isn't really satisfied, for one reason or another, with any of the options she's considered, so she goes on doing what she's been doing.

REGULAR CAR MAINTENANCE: On the issue of Whitney's pumping gas, Alison has decided that you pick your battles, and this isn't one that's profoundly important.

Neale's Comments

AFTER-SCHOOL PICKUP: Alison has fallen into the "just wouldn't feel right unless I do it myself" trap here.

There's a scene in the classic movie *The African Queen* where Humphrey Bogart and Katharine Hepburn are going downriver on an ancient steam-powered barge. A wrench that has fallen into the boat's boiler gets stuck, and Humphrey Bogart has to kick the boiler until he dislodges the wrench—otherwise, the engine will explode. Hepburn asks him why he doesn't take the boiler apart and remove the wrench. Bogey replies that the old boiler is pretty close to all he has in the world and then says, "I kinda like kickin' it."

That's Alison. Her phone calls from whatever part of the country she happens to be in aren't the best way of solving the problem, but they give her a sense of day-to-day participation in her kids' lives when she's away.

Actually, if Alison weren't spending her time on making phone calls to set up rides, she could be using that time to actually participate in her kids' lives—by calling the kids and talking to them.

But life isn't always neatly logical. Would you want to be the one to give Alison this little pearl of wisdom? I wouldn't. Don't forget that Alison's kids are at the age where they have a very clear sense of what telephones are for. They're for talking to your friends, not your parents.

I would, on the other hand, have no trouble telling Alison that she shouldn't worry about what the neighbors think.

The truth is, Alison's not a traveling salesperson or a touring golf pro. Business trips are an important part of her job, but she doesn't spend most of her life on the road. Travel is a sometime thing for her, which makes it all the more a good idea that she have a simple plan in place so she doesn't have to improvise every time.

Alison should go for the cab service.

REGULAR CAR MAINTENANCE: It's easy to tell Alison that she should be a woman instead of a mouse, that she should stand up to her daughter and darn well make her pump gas, but I wouldn't be too hard on her here. Perhaps it isn't profoundly important. We know our own kids, and our own tolerance levels, better than anyone else does.

Alison has another thing working for her here—her awareness of imminent personnel turnover. She lives in a state where the driving age for kids is sixteen, and pretty soon Whitney is going to want a driver's license. At that point, the whole transportation issue will enter a new phase, which will include new ground rules involving automotive principles and responsibilities.

At that point, Whitney starts pumping gas.

• • •

This raises an interesting point of definition: just what constitutes outsourcing in a home context?

▶ If you hire a professional (a cab company), that's definitely outsourcing.

▶ If you hire a friend or a neighbor on a contractual basis, even a verbal one, that's outsourcing.

▶ If you join or organize a co-op, where you drive once a week and others drive on designated days, this is not outsourcing anymore, it's just co-oping. This can work for certain situations, but it's not an option for Alison in this case because no such co-op exists in her neighborhood—and even if one did, she couldn't be relied on to take a regular turn.

▶ If you call a bunch of friends and try to find someone who'll do it, you've moved totally away from outsourcing. You've just created an extended version of your somewhat disorganized family.

Outsourcing doesn't just mean getting someone else to do it. This is important to remember if you're thinking, "Oh, yeah, outsourcing—I've tried that, and it didn't work."

Don't forget. In the workplace, we expect things to work. If they don't work, we don't just dismiss them; we analyze why they didn't work. Was the whole plan flawed or could it be modified?

In the home, all too often, we don't necessarily expect things to work, so when they don't work, we don't analyze. We tend to say, "Ah, yes, that's just how things are."

We don't have to approach problems in the home expecting all our solutions to fail. If we expect to succeed, and we analyze problems in the home with that expectation, we actually can solve a lot more than we might think.

If we're clear on just how outsourcing works, we can

consider it for some household tasks. If it doesn't work, we can analyze and understand why not. Did outsourcing create more problems than it solved? Or did we just use the wrong subcontractor?

Time Management

What needs to be done?

Trevor's sports and other activities mean that he has a lot of appointments that are scheduled for him and that won't wait for him.

Whitney doesn't have the same kind of built-in structure to her activities, but she's no less passionate about them. She does things with her friends. She's begun doing volunteer work, like reading to a blind neighbor once or twice a week. She has unscheduled impulses—a movie or a concert or an art exhibit that she just *has* to see.

How does it get done?

Alison's had a system, and for a while it seemed like a pretty good system. She had a three-month calendar up in the kitchen, and on it she put all the things that were regularly scheduled events. Some of them, like birthdays, got inked in automatically, and others got put in as they came up. A lot of Trevor's dates, like his Little League games or his soccer games, were scheduled way in advance.

Whitney hasn't found it so easy: "How was I supposed to know that *Titanic* was going to be so good I'd have to go see it five times?" Or: "Who's going to tell me that housekeeper was going to be out of town *and* we were going to come to a chapter in *Lord of the Rings* that was so exciting she just had to have me come over three evenings in a row to read to her?" Or: "Well, yes, if I'd just gotten a walk-on part in the play, I only would have had to show up for a couple of rehearsals. But I got the *lead!* Am I such a bad daughter because other people think I'm talented?"

"You could still do better," Alison tells her. "Everything doesn't have to take us by surprise at the last minute. If you even wrote your plans in two or three days in advance, maybe we'd be able to make sure we could get you a ride or get you what you needed."

"Yeah, right, *maybe*," Whitney snaps back at her.

And things aren't getting better. Whitney is still surprising her with last-minute plans, still getting furious when Alison can't accommodate her. Alison is still getting frustrated by what appears to be Whitney's casual, uncaring attitude toward family organization.

What are the other options?

Alison is starting to think wistfully along the "maybe you *can* fire your family" line, but since you can't, what *are* the other options?

What would she do with an employee who was constantly disruptive of the company's schedule?

Why would she keep such an employee?

There would have to be a reason. You wouldn't have someone, or keep someone, for no reason.

And a light goes on in Alison's head. What *is* the reason for fourteen-year-old Whitney's being part of the family's personnel team? Is it possible that Whitney can't see a reason, that she feels as though she doesn't belong?

Alison remembers just a few years ago, when the dynamic was reversed. Both the kids were going to a local private school that had a wonderful reputation for encouraging creativity and independence from Montessori-based preschool through the sixth grade. Whitney was one of the stars of the school. She reveled in its creative freedom. She excelled in art, in drama, in academics. Trevor was sullen, uncooperative, a discipline problem.

Finally, in desperation, Alison withdrew him from the school and put him in a military school. Suddenly, Trevor began to flower. He loved the discipline. He loved being told this was right and that was wrong. After two years, Alison put him in the local public school, and his inner discipline carried over.

Alison's company has a research-and-development department. It includes a couple of people who are visionary, creative, inspired, and disorganized. The company makes allowances for their disorganization because it understands that you don't advance into the future without a few individuals who color outside the lines.

You need creative individuals to develop products that will advance you into the future. In Alison's home, the individuals are the future product, and it's their own strengths—creativity or organization—that will ultimately create those products.

Alison realizes that she has to find a system of organizing that is flexible enough to meet the needs and the strengths of both her children, as well as her own needs. The current system works well for Trevor, but she needs a system that will bring Whitney more into the picture.

What are the pros and cons?

The main advantage to the current system is that it's a really good basis for organizing the family to make use of limited resources—that is, one car, one driver.

The main disadvantage is that it's not entirely working. There's still chaos, and what's worse, it's causing at least as much family friction as it's preventing.

What's the choice?

What if the three-month appointment calendar weren't so much the center of the family's organization? And what if

Alison included Whitney a lot more in the scheduling process?

That's a scary thought, at first. Alison floats it by her sister, who asks, "And if you were managing a henhouse, who would you have making the schedule? The fox?"

"Hey, wait a second." Alison laughs. "Whitney isn't on a secret mission to destroy this family from within. She's part of the family, and if it's not working for her, it's not working."

Alison sits down with Whitney, assuring her that she wants to know what Whitney thinks and she is prepared to listen. She starts really drawing Whitney out about what she thinks the family needs.

The first thing she knows, they're in the middle of a discussion of family projects and privacy issues, about how important it is to be able to feel free to make spur-of-the-moment decisions, and how it's also important to keep some kind of family schedule. They talk about family vacations and working together as a family on volunteer projects.

Whitney admits that she knows it's important to let people know at least some of what she's doing in advance, and Alison assures her that she understands how things come up at the last minute, and that she doesn't think one activity is better or more important than another just because it's scheduled farther in advance. She assures Whitney that she won't choose Trevor's soccer game over her school play just because it went up on the calendar first.

"You know, Mom," Whitney says, "I'd have a lot easier time with this scheduling business if it weren't so dumb-looking."

"What do you suggest?" Alison asks. "I can't just ask you every day if you have something coming up. That would drive both of us crazy."

"You could call my friends and ask them." Whitney giggles. "They always know what I'm doing."

"Or I could E-mail them," Alison says. "Wait! That's it! Why don't we E-mail our schedules to each other. You're always E-mailing your friends, anyway—you could just cut and paste the parts where you're telling them about plans to do stuff and send it to me. Trevor could do it, too . . . he's just learning how to use computers. Then I could coordinate it on a master list and E-mail it back to everyone."

"Or I could coordinate it," says Whitney. "Mom, that is so cool!"

Neale's Comments

There's nothing a mother likes to hear better than "Mom, that is so cool!"

Letting Whitney coordinate, even by E-mail, would be carrying sharing the responsibility one step too far, and Alison is smart enough to know that.

She's done everything right here, and she's picked up some very valuable insights. Like your workplace, your home is populated by personnel who are there for a reason. The difference is, in the workplace you identify the job and then find the employee. At home, the employee is a given; you have to make sure you understand and appreciate the role each individual is playing.

Chapter 10

Office Techniques at Home

The projects you create and see through to fruition at home will be different from the projects you're used to at work, but the techniques and tools of undertaking and finishing a successful project will be remarkably similar.

At work your projects are, at bottom, governed by the profit motive. That's why they call it the bottom line. If you're an owner or a partner, you're directly affected by every dime of profit or loss. If you're management, or if you're labor, you're working for your own advancement, and your own advancement is tied directly, or very closely, to your company's bottom line.

At home, you and your family are your own bottom line. Your goals are the enrichment, the spiritual fulfillment, the physical health, and the intellectual, moral, and creative growth of your children into responsible, mature adults.

Well, that's the serious end of it. You can toss in a few other goals, too: to have a few laughs; to make and share those memories that come from the unplanned parts of life.

But as different as the goals are, the techniques and philosophies are transferable.

Here are a few of the key business techniques you should consider in turning your family into a smooth-running team.

The Family Meeting

There are three things you want out of a family meeting:

1. You want all members of the family to take part and to feel as though their input is appreciated.
2. You want all members of the family to come out of the meeting with a clear sense of what they can expect and what is expected of them.
3. You want to come out of the meeting with things decided (at least mostly) the way you want them.

I've said that she who controls the agenda controls the meeting, and that's true. But you also can expect to get more of what you want out of a meeting if you:

▶ Control the physical setup of a meeting
▶ Go into the meeting knowing what you want to get out of it—what you're willing to concede, what you'd like to achieve, and what you absolutely won't budge on.

Control the Physical Setup

When there are huge, high stakes for a meeting—a summit conference between two superpowers, for example—weeks can be spent on premeeting meetings and arguing about things like the size of the table and the placement of chairs.

Most of us tend to think of this sort of jockeying for advantage as more than a little excessive, but the logistical details of a family meeting do make a difference.

Picture a meeting being held at your dining room table, with pencils and notebooks set out neatly at everyone's place. Imagine that the meeting has been called for seven P.M. sharp, and that everyone in the family has been reminded of the time via a written memo on the morning of the meeting.

Got that? Now picture another meeting. This one is held in the family room. It's been called for "after school on Thursday" or for "when your dad and I get home from work."

What's the difference in the mental picture you have of these two meetings?

I tried this out in a seminar on family management, and here's how it went.

Cindy: For the first one, I see everybody in the family arriving just at seven, or maybe five minutes before. I see them coming in and sitting down, and everyone greeting each other politely: "Hello, Mom . . . Hello, Jack . . . How are you, Richard? . . . Good evening, Dad."

I see myself dressed up in a business suit, the way I'd look at the office. Actually, come to think of it, I see everyone sort of dressed up.

Neale: Have you told everyone to dress up for the meeting?

Cindy: I don't think so. I sort of pictured it that if you made the meeting formal like that, everyone would naturally respond to it by dressing up.

Betta: But you could make it a rule, couldn't you? This is a formal family meeting, and I expect everyone to treat it with the respect you'd treat any other formal meeting.

Ginny: You might have a written agenda. You could type it up on the computer, make as many copies as you needed, and put one by everyone's pencil and notebook.

Neale: Would you do that for the second meeting—the one where you all get together in the family room?

Ginny: You could make up copies of an agenda, I suppose, but where would you put them? Maybe in a pile on the table next to the onion dip.

Neale: What else would be different?

Cindy: Everything. If you set a time like "after school" or "after work" you're not going to have everyone showing up just at seven. They'll be drifting in, and you'll probably end up by having to go and find someone.

Ginny: I certainly don't see everyone dressed up for this one.

Neale: Which one is better?

Ginny: The formal one.

Betta: You'd get more accomplished, and not just because everyone would be there on time. If you keep the meeting businesslike, everyone knows it's serious.

Erica: I don't know . . . wouldn't it make a difference what you were trying to accomplish?

Neale: What do you mean?

Erica: Maybe you might have a reason for not wanting the meeting to be too formal. Maybe you might feel there's more of a chance for creative solutions to problems if everyone feels more at ease to toss their two cents in.

Ginny: Even for the informal meeting, there are some formal rules you'd absolutely have to stick to. Nothing is allowed to interrupt the meeting. No phone calls. Let your machine pick it up. And if you or your kids have friends who are in the habit of just dropping by unannounced—

Erica: Or in-laws.

Ginny: Or in-laws. Call them and warn them in advance that there'll be no stopping by tonight. Then put a note up on the door saying come back later.

Neale: So can we say that, in general, the structure of the meeting depends on what you want to accomplish in the meeting?

Erica: Maybe it does. And maybe it depends on who your family is, too? I always think it's a good thing to keep people on their toes, and one way I've done that at work is by sometimes going a little against the grain. If I think my project team is going a little too much by the book, I'll hold a very informal meeting with soda and pizza. Maybe I'll take it somewhere outside the office. On the other hand, if I think the group might be getting a little too lax, I'll be more formal with my meetings.

It's important that your family members know that family meetings are for all of them and that anyone can call a family meeting. As far as meetings are concerned, they're definitely board of directors and not employees. But you're still the CEO, the keeper of the vision.

Know What You Want to Get from the Meeting

Without a clear sense of vision, a meeting can start to be about itself. The topic under discussion goes off on tangents.

The most effective business meetings begin with the boss articulating the meeting's purpose. When I was in the banking business, I used to do even more than that. I made

up little laminated cards with the company's mission statement and gave them to all my employees. Whenever the
meeting started to get off track (which could happen
quickly), I'd bring everyone back to earth by saying "Let's
take out the cards, read them all together, and remember
why we're here."

Remember, your job is, first, to facilitate the discussion;
second, to create a space where the discussion can actually
take place; and third, to bring everyone into the discussion
and make people understand that it's important to contribute.

There are other good reasons for keeping the meeting
focused. If you know what's most important to you, you can
graciously concede less-important points. If you know that
you have to cut back the budget for this year's family vacation so that you'll have money to send Mom and Dad on a
cruise for their fiftieth wedding anniversary, don't get locked
into an argument over whether it's better to spend the vacation fishing or hiking.

> *Alison remembers a family meeting in which she had to
> bring up a subject that she knew was going to cause contro-
> versy—the decision to send Trevor to a private military
> school. The school was expensive, and in order to afford it
> they were going to have to make some major adjustments to
> their budget, taking money away from many other places it
> had been designated—including some that had been ear-
> marked for Whitney.*
>
> *Whitney was indignant: "What do you mean, you're
> going to be taking all our money and spending it on Trevor?"*
>
> *Alison held firm: "It's something that has to be done,
> it's not something frivolous."*
>
> *"Well, I want to get my share, too. It's not fair that
> everything goes to Trevor."*
>
> *By this time, Trevor was starting to get into it, too:
> "Oh, yeah? We pay for your school, too."*

"Not as much as yours."

"Well, who says I want to go? It's not my decision, so it doesn't count against my money."

"It's our money," Alison reminded them. "We're a family, first, last, and always, remember? And remember our mission statement: To make a place in which healthy, happy, and responsible growth can flourish."

"Well, this isn't going to make me happy," Whitney said.

"But it's the responsible thing to do," Alison told her. "And it's necessary for Trevor's growth."

"So you're saying that you can pick and choose in our mission statement? Trevor's growth means more than my happiness?"

"It's not your happiness that's at stake here, dear. How do you really feel right now?"

"I'm darn mad."

"Yes, and that's not so bad. Mad isn't the same as unhappy. We can get mad and still support each other. Sometimes one of us really needs something, and then we all pitch in. That doesn't mean we give up making decisions as a family or that we have to sacrifice everything that's important. Let's take a look at our budget. We'll see how much we have to cut, and we'll all work together at deciding where we'll make the cuts."

Alison would have made it explicitly clear that the first cuts in the budget would come from other activities or expenses that were largely for Trevor, but she didn't have to. Trevor took the lead, pointing out first that since he'd be wearing school uniforms, he could cut down a lot on his clothing allowance for school.

When they got to the budget for their vacation trip that year, they agreed that it could be cut by a quarter. "And what about if Whitney decides where we're going this year—and plans the trip?" Alison said.

"That's fair," Trevor agreed.

"Not every compensation has to be monetary," Whitney added.

Neale's Comment

Alison is right on. There are going to be times when you simply have to rally around. If you're responsible for a large company, and your Midwestern sales area suddenly comes up
way short of its quota, you don't decide that the Midwestern
division will just have to give up its salaries, you adjust the
budget company-wide to reflect the numbers. You wouldn't
put up with one regional manager saying, "It was those guys'
fault—why should we have to share the responsibility?"

And if you're responsible for a small office, and someone gets sick and can't come in, you don't say, "No problem—we'll just keep going without that person's work
getting done." You make sure that everyone chips in and
shoulders a little more of that responsibility all around.

Of course, kids are going to bicker to some extent. They
are kids, and not executives (executives are childish in other
ways). But it is also possible to make them understand that
things happen.

You'd also know what to do if something terribly serious
happened. If one of your children suffered a serious illness,
there'd be no question that everyone in the family would
have to make adjustments. You'd try to make certain that you
compensated your other kids, whether it was with time or
something you spent money on, just as Alison will try to
make sure that she does something special for Whitney. But
the first step is making it clear that what has to be, has to be.

When You Can't Negotiate

We all have the urge to shield our kids from some of the
harsh realities of life, but that's not always possible. Some
things can't be changed, and they can't be negotiated.

Kids don't always know the difference. They are passionate negotiators, and they tend not to understand why they can't have things their way.

It's important to know when you can't negotiate. If you're clear in your own mind that certain things simply have to be the way they are, then you can make it clear. It's particularly important here to use the office as a model. Don't be defensive; don't get into an argument. Clarity and decisiveness are the best tools you can use in stating a non-negotiable position.

Project Manager: Linda Ann Goodwin, fifty, executive vice president, Fleet Bank. Mom of Nina, twenty-seven.

I had been raised to believe I was supposed to be married and supported by my husband, but it didn't work out that way. I first had to learn to be the breadwinner of the family; and then, when my marriage broke up, I had to learn how to be financially independent and support my daughter on my own.

This all came in stages. The first stage was realizing that my husband wasn't going to "find himself," and if I wanted money coming in, I'd have to get a job. The second came when he finally decided he couldn't find himself within the confines of marriage and moved out. Nina was eight then, and the job I'd had involved a lot of travel.

Just at that time, the company wanted to promote me to a position in marketing where I'd be on the road nearly all the time. I would have had a hard time accepting that even with a househusband at home; as a single parent, I absolutely could not do it. I went to the company, laid out a different plan for them, and they accepted it. I moved into a position where the travel could be kept to a minimum.

Still, there was a certain amount of travel, and I had to adapt to it. One of the most important lessons I'd learned in business is that you have to be honest with yourself. You can't be everywhere at once, and you can't do everything yourself. The idea that it takes a village to raise a child never came as much of a surprise to me, because I already knew that it takes a village to run a multibillion-dollar corporation.

I wasn't able to be at a lot of important events for Nina. I regretted it, but there wasn't any way around it. So I didn't promise Nina that I'd be there and then stand her up at the last moment; I always told her that there would be things I couldn't do.

We did other things together. Fortunately, Nina was interested in what I did, so she'd come with me to spend a morning doing research at the company library, then we'd spend a long lunch hour in the park and go for ice cream.

Nina, who's now a successful businesswoman on her own, has memories very similar to her mother's: "Of course, I was disappointed that Mom couldn't be at every soccer game or school play, but I understood because Mom was always honest with me. I felt that I was helping by being supportive, the same way that Mom helped me. I always knew that Mom loved me and that she would include me in everything she could. When I went with Mom to do research, that was one of my favorite things, because she never made me feel like I was in the way or just tagging along—we really did it together."

Chapter 11

The Kid Projects

Your biggest long-term project is your kids.

When we're planning our families, it's pretty close to impossible to have any sense of the scope of each child project. It's pretty close to impossible to have any sense of the time it'll take, which is natural, because time is the slipperiest, most unmeasurable thing there is. Time isn't measured by hours and minutes, it's measured by what happens in it and how it feels to us. When we're pregnant, nine months seems like an eternity, and the last few weeks of it seems longer than the first seven months put together.

There are days that we think will never end, when we have one sick toddler and one hyperactive one. There are nights that stretch on forever, when there's a teenager out there who hasn't called to say he'll be late.

So you're going to have this creature around the house for the next eighteen years? That sounds like a process, if there ever was one. But process is defined as something that's routine, day after day. It's the same old problems, the same old solutions.

Raising your children is not going to be the same never-ending process for eighteen years, because that creature who moves in on your life for the next eighteen years is not going to be the same creature throughout that eighteen years. You won't be changing diapers that whole time. Your kids are actually an ideal laboratory for testing out techniques for turning process into project: the infant project, the toddler project, the adolescent project, until they've left home.

In an era when we've come to take it as a given that women don't have to be bound by any of the old stereotypes, we can still lay some new traps for ourselves. We know that not every woman is cut out to be married, and words like *spinster* and *old maid* have pretty much disappeared from contemporary vocabularies. We've learned that some women aren't cut out to be stay-at-home moms, and some women aren't cut out to be mothers at all. We've also learned that some women do feel best staying at home with their kids, and if they can work out the finances, that's great, too.

But what they don't always tell you is that being a mom is not a one-note process, requiring the same set of skills, instincts, and personality traits throughout the job.

This means that parenthood has its ups and downs (no big surprise here!). Sooner or later each one of us is going to run into a situation for which she seems hopelessly ill-equipped. And since we already know that time has a particularly sadistic habit of virtually standing still whenever it gets to a part that we'd just as soon be over with as quickly as possible, we can count on time standing dead still at these times. We can't remember the beginning, and we can't see the end. During these periods any one of us is likely to fall prey to a thought like "My God, do you suppose it's me? Can I be one of those women who's not cut out to be a mother?"

Relax. Motherhood covers such a wide range of skills and instincts, aptitudes, and demands on temperament that it should come as no surprise that none of us is likely to be equally good at all of them.

Why should this be a problem? Where is it written that anyone has to be equally good at everything she takes on? The reality is that the job skills you bring to the toddler project are not at all the same ones you'll use for the prepubescent project.

And while a mom-CEO has to be a generalist rather than a specialist (moms are the greatest generalists of all), the inescapable truth is that you're going to be more skilled at some projects than others.

This is not a bad thing, and it's not unusual. This is worth repeating because it trips up a lot of moms. It's not unusual to be better at one area of parenting, or one era of parenting, than another.

How many of us suffer from Mommy Guilt because we're not perfect? Because we like taking a group of Cub Scouts on a nature walk better than we like changing diapers, or because we like putting powder on a baby's bottom better than we like taking our twelve-year-old on a paintball weekend?

Everyone is like that. And it's all right to be like that. But you need to be aware of it, so that you don't fall too much in love with one project. You might have a natural gift for relating to five-year-olds, but you have to accept that the five-year-old project is going to end and that your child will not be satisfied with staying five years old "just a little longer."

There's nothing wrong with having some management skills that are stronger than others. But there's also nothing wrong with realizing and adjusting it to it either, which you can sometimes do by outsourcing (line up Uncle Irv to take Jason to the paintball weekend) and sometimes by awareness and preparation.

(P.S. This is equally true whether you're a working mom or a stay-at-home mom. If you're not the kind of mom who'll make it a priority to rush home from work for a paintball weekend, you're not the kind of mom who will throw herself wholeheartedly into paintball as a stay-at-home mom, either. So just forget the guilt part, okay?)

What Do They Do?

Here's a checklist to make up for yourself. For each age group, write down a list of all the characteristics of kids that age for each sex (where applicable; there's not much difference with babies, but that changes fast).

Make a list of everything kids do at that age—fun stuff, awful stuff, heartwarming stuff, heartrending stuff, stuff that makes more work for you, stuff that gives you the opportunity to do things you love to do.

If your list isn't complete, don't worry. It isn't supposed to be. Nobody's list will ever be complete. That's not the point. I've put in a few samples here, but make your own list.

Then make an assessment of how you feel about each of these characteristics, on a scale of 1 to 4:

1. Love it
2. Can handle it
3. Would just as soon not
4. Yuk!

Age group	What they do	Your rating
Babies	Eat	
	Get diapers changed	
	Get bathed	
	Respond	
	Crawl	
	Begin to talk	

Toddlers	Get read to
	Start learning to read
	Play indoors
	Play outdoors
	Watch TV
	Computers
	Parties
	Play dates
Preschool	Classes
	Alone activities
	Discipline
	Reading
	Puzzles—hand and brain games
Grade school	Discipline
	Going out without you
	Homework
	Being driven around
	Holiday activities
	Class field trips
	More alone time
Preteen	A lot of alone time
	More discipline
	Lot of chauffeuring
	Boy-girl things
Teenage	Serious discipline problems
	Driving
	College prep
	Serious boy-girl stuff
	Very little parental involvement

This list isn't meant to be scientific or exhaustive. Your list will be longest around the age that your kids are now; for ages older than your kids have reached yet, you'll just be guessing, or drawing on your own childhood memories. But you'll have created a pretty good self-portrait of the experiences of child-rearing that you're most drawn to and the ones you see yourself as having the most trouble with.

Have some friends do this exercise, too, and compare

lists. It'll remind you of things you've forgotten on your own list. If you're like many of us, you might tend to be too hard on yourself, and focus on the things you're not good at, or not drawn to. Your friends' lists might remind you of some of the things you do shine at.

We're all strange and wonderful creatures, and we're drawn to what we're drawn to. One friend told me, "I always thought *this* was probably a little weird, but I loved changing diapers. I just love little babies—I think they're the most magical things in the world. And I love all the human, natural things they do. And I loved knowing I was making my kids feel dry and powdered and comfy. I miss it now that they're bigger."

It's not weird. Child rearing is a magical and wonderful thing. The parts that aren't magical to you are magical to someone—and *vive la différence!*

Proactive Priorities

This list will give you a basis on which to start budgeting the time you spend with your kids. Make sure that you allow plenty of time for doing the things you like to do best. The things you like to do best are, for the most part, the things that you *will* do best, and dollars to doughnuts says that your kids will enjoy them the most, too.

Okay, that part's easy. Your first proactive step is to ensure that you have the most fun possible with your kids.

Aha. I hear a voice, and it sounds like a mother's voice, saying, What if the thing that's the most fun for you is taking the kids to Disneyland? That's the way you modern women are. You just want all of the fun and none of the responsibilities. You've made your choice—career over family. That's why your children have to raise themselves.

We all hear that voice, don't we? It's a very hard one to

ignore. It says if we're running our lives well, according to a proactive plan that works for us, if we're having fun with our families and success in our work, then we must be doing something wrong. We must be selfish creatures.

Relax. Take a look back at your checklist. Does it say:

Taking the kids to Disney World: Love it

Everything else: Yuk!

If it doesn't, then this voice of gloom is one that we can tune out.

We are involved with our kids in a variety of ways. We like doing their homework with them, or we like reading to them. We like teaching them to cook and take care of the kitchen, or we like running family meetings and seeing our kids take part in the decision-making process.

Follow your joy. It's the best way to build a business, it's the best way to build a home.

But it's not the whole story. There's a lot about every job that you don't like, but it still has to be done.

Sure, but does it have to be done by you?

Yes, some of it does. There's no way any organization is *only* going to move forward on the basis of doing things that you like, and there's no way that you can totally avoid all the blah stuff, the yucky stuff, the stuff you're uncomfortable with, and the just plain drudgery.

But that's never been our problem, has it? We're none of us likely to run away from our responsibilities, especially the ones we enjoy the least. We're much more likely to square our shoulders and face up to them. We think that's what we have to do. We've been lectured, until it becomes a voice inside us lecturing ourselves, that this is what responsible women do. The more of the drudgery we take on, according to this voice, the better we are as moms.

But if we step back and look at it from the perspective of what we know of life beyond that tunnel vision that can sometimes afflict us as moms, what kind of a way is that to run a business? Are you judged in your performance reviews, or at the bottom line of your ledger, on the basis of how much of the drudge work you shouldered? No—you're judged by how well you made your department run, how well you functioned as part of a project team and got the project completed. It's time that we applied those same standards to ourselves in the home. Rather than just accept that there's a lot of routine involved in running a home and that the more we shoulder the more virtuous we are, let's be proactive.

First, look back at your list and remind yourself once again that nothing lasts forever. That the seemingly endless process of motherhood chores isn't really one endless chore; it's a whole series of different situations. It might be true that woman's work is never done, but actually, nobody's work is ever done. Women's *projects* can be planned, started, and finished.

Now look at the items you've marked "Would just as soon not" or "Yuk!" and start separating them out into two categories:

1. I have to do this myself.
2. I can outsource this.

For the first category, for everything you've decided that you have to do yourself, ask another question:

Why?

This isn't a multiple-choice answer. For this one, you have to sit down and write at least a sentence explaining why you have to do it yourself. Then go back and read these

over. Who is speaking? Is it the voice of the confident, pro-
ject-making businesswoman, or is it the voice that still wor-
ries about that *they* think you should be doing?

Sometimes, at work or at home, the clear-sighted managerial voice will end up saying "Yes, there's no way around
it. I do have to do this yucky stuff." But that managerial
voice can also identify the chore as a project, can estimate its
duration, and can make a plan for it that might very well include assembling a team to share the workload.

Other times, you'll realize it's not the clear-sighted
managerial voice speaking and that this is a chore you *can*
move to the outsourcing column,

Next, make a new checklist of house and yard things
that are not especially kid-related, and separate them the
same way, from *Love it* to *Yuk!*

You can think about outsourcing these things, too.

In my family, we've streamlined our holiday planning a
lot, preferring to concentrate on the closeness of family and
reaching out to include people who are alone on the holidays. But we still do have some family ceremony, and there
are some family heirlooms that we bring out, including some
silver candlesticks and servers. The thing about silver is, it
needs to be polished, and the thing about polishing silver is, I
really hate to do it. I hate the smell of the silver polish; I hate
everything about it. I used to tell everyone that the candlesticks were pewter so I wouldn't have to polish them. When
we talked about what really mattered for the holidays, I was
secretly hoping everyone would say, "We certainly don't
need all that old silver stuff."

What my kids said, instead, was, "We don't need all the
formal stuff, but it's really nice to have some of it. Why don't
we go on using the silver candlesticks? *We'll* polish them; we
love to do that."

Who knew? I couldn't have imagined that anyone
would love to polish silver. But I'm delighted that they do,

not only because the candlesticks really do look beautiful, but because it's such a tangible expression of their commitment to the family.

Project Manager: Susan Blefary, thirty-one, receptionist. Mom of Jenna, seven; Ronna, five; and Dara, three.

Whenever I get together with my friends, one thing everyone else always complains about is having to drive with little kids.

I figured I was odd because I liked it.

But what's not to like? I like to drive, and I like to talk. I like talking to little kids. They're so smart, they're so curious, they're learning things all the time. And when you're driving is one of the best times to talk to them, because they're in one place. Heck, they're strapped in!

When you're driving, you're in a classroom on wheels. Everything is a lesson. What does that sign say? S . . . T . . . O . . . P. Can you sound it out? Can you read the billboards? What's the number on that sign? Five! What's that mean? It means it's five miles to town! I have all my kids reading and doing their numbers just driving around town.

Like I said, I just kept quiet about this for a while, because I figured my friends would have me committed if I kept talking about it. But then I realized I could barter carpooling for other chores. I thought it was neat when other moms started telling me, "My kid knows his numbers now! I can't believe it!" So I'm having a good time, I'm actually helping kids, and I can trade for baby-sitting time so I can go back and take courses at the community college.

Chapter 12

Budget Projects

What part of making a family budget should be a project that involves the whole family?

All of it.

What family members should be brought into the budget-making process?

All of them.

Even your littlest ones can be apprentices in the job of family money management, and they should be part of family meetings in which budgets are discussed from as early as they're able to sit still and follow a conversation. They'll understand as much as they need to, and they'll start to get familiar with concepts, particularly the concept that you can't have everything. It's one thing to tell a four-year-old that money doesn't grow on trees, but he's not going to see it as a finite substance when he sees you reach into your wallet and pull it out when you need it—or if you're not pulling out cash, you're pulling out those "little magic plastic cards." However, when he sees the whole family sitting in a room, and going over lists of numbers together, and agreeing that, sure enough, we won't be able to afford to put in the new rec room *and* go to Disney World this year, and weighing the pros and cons of each decision—he might not understand the details but he'll start to realize that these choices are real ones.

Work for Pay

This is the cornerstone of every family financial responsibility project. Kids should understand early that there is a relationship between work and money, between money and responsibility.

Anyone who's listened to me talk on radio or TV, or been to any of my seminars, or read anything I've written, knows that I believe in the value of having kids work for the money they get. I believe that an allowance should always be part of a larger financial awareness and financial responsibility project.

But not everyone realizes that I extend this philosophy to kids as young as three years old.

"What can a three-year-old really do?" I get asked over and over again. "Do you really expect a little toddler to help keep house?" And, "I've heard you say, 'No work, no pay.' Can you really hold a three-year-old to that?"

The answers are, a three-year-old can't do very much, and if you're expecting your three-year-old to be the difference between a messy house and an immaculate one, you're going to be very disappointed. In fact, if you expect an immaculate house when you have toddlers, you might be disappointed, and you *might*—although, of course, there are women who can do anything—be allocating your resources in the wrong way if you try too hard to achieve it. That generally means doing everything yourself, because between you and a toddler, there's no question who's going to be the more efficient housekeeper.

Part of the expected and planned-for results of the toddler project should include a certain amount of imperfection in housekeeping. Another part should be the development of a child with a sense of responsibility.

And no, I am not advocating "tough love" for three-year-olds. "No work, no pay" is a good rule, but it's an especially good rule if everyone always works and everyone always gets paid. In the case of a three-year-old, you'll go with him as he does his chores—dusting the low end tables in the living room, for example—talking him through the jobs and making sure that they're done, then going with him to put the star next to his name on the allowance chart/chore list on the refrigerator. Letting your toddler sort socks from the clean laundry into pairs is not only a chore, it's a learning game.

As kids get older, the work-for-pay jobs need to become more challenging. At every age, your children should know that:

▶ The jobs aren't just make-work. They really make a difference in the running of the household, and it matters whether they are done or not.

▶ The jobs will demand something of them. They'll be a challenge, and that challenge will increase with their age and ability to handle challenges.

▶ They will not get paid for what they're supposed to do: getting good grades, being polite to people, or what I call "Citizen of the Household Chores," which are those chores (they'll vary from household to household) that everyone in the family should simply be expected to chip in and do.

There can be other, nonmonetary rewards for good grades and active participation in Citizen of the Household projects. We've learned this from business, too. Study after study in business has shown that employees respond as much or more to approval as they do to monetary bonuses.

People like to be praised; they like to be recognized for their intrinsic value. And if this approach works for your business associates and employees, it certainly ought to work for your family, which is an institution that's so much more deeply invested in emotional ties.

One reward that works well in business is some kind of Employee of the Month Award. You couldn't institute a Child of the Month Award. But you can create a Pride Board, which I did when my kids were younger. This is a place—it can be a board in the kitchen or a book in the living room—where, every week, your kids write down something they've done, or something about themselves, that they're proud of. There's always something to be proud of, and it's important to let your kids know that those are the things you care most about and they should be the things that they care more about.

Work for pay is not only the cornerstone of teaching kids responsibility, it's also the cornerstone of teaching them budgeting and financial management.

For years, I've been teaching financial management for children using what I originally developed as the three-jar system—and what I have now expanded into the four-jar system. Simply put (since I've written about this at greater length in other books), these are:

> ▶ One jar for Charity. This is the new jar, but it's always been part of my philosophy of teaching a child financial and social responsibility. We're part of a larger community, and we need to remember that in that community there are people who need our

help. Our children need to know that. They need to know that there is always something we can do to help, that there is always something they can do to help.

Your child should put aside 10 percent of any money she earns, or receives as gifts, for charity. This comes first. Then the remainder of the money is divided evenly into the other three jars.

▶ One jar for Quick Cash. This is your child's discretionary income. She can spend it any time she wants, on anything she wants (as long as it's not something disallowed in your family).

▶ One jar for Medium-Term Savings. Your child can save up for some purchase of his own choosing— something that will cost more than one week's pay will allow for. For very little ones, this should be a toy he can save up for in two or three weeks. Older kids should be encouraged to set their goals longer and learn more about deferred gratification.

▶ One jar for Long-Term Savings. This is for college. From early childhood, the concept that she carries part of the responsibility for her own college education should be part of your child's awareness. She should grow up with this as a part of who she is.

The four-jar system is the beginning of a child's understanding of budgeting.

The Family Budget

How much should a child be involved in family finances and the family budget? I believe that this is not an area of life that needs to be hidden. Why should it be? You'd never be able to function in a business in which you didn't have at least a general understanding of the budget and how your part of it fit in with the total package. And a family is a much closer unit than any business.

It's odd. In a time when people seem to have no compunction about going on television and discussing what used to be considered the most embarrassing and personal details of their sex lives, we still shrink back in horror from discussing anything about our financial lives. "That's too personal." "That's private." "That's nobody's business but mine and my family's."

And frequently, it's even more private than that. We won't even discuss it with our families.

Why not? There seem to be a variety of reasons. Sometimes, we want to protect our children from "growing up too fast," having to learn about the harsh financial realities of life. Sometimes, we don't want our children to know how little we make, because we're afraid they'll think less of us. Sometimes, we don't want our children to know how *much* we make, because we're afraid they'll want us to buy them more. Sometimes, we just don't want to talk about finances because that's what we were taught: it's something that nice people don't talk about.

But I'm saying that's wrong. Working out a budget should be a family project. It brings the family together in important ways. It gives your kids a sense of the value of things, and of the very real problems of making ends meet, and the decisions that have to be made. It gives them a share of family responsibility.

Here are some of the things that should go into a family budgeting project:

▶ **Bill paying:** There's no reason why, when your kids get to be eleven or twelve, they can't be included in the family bill-paying project.

▶ **Vacation planning:** This is another project that can involve the whole family in every aspect of planning. It shouldn't just be limited to "where do you want to go?" If you involve the whole family in the budgeting for your vacation, you can also then involve them in a discussion of value received for their vacation dollar.

How much of the vacation budget will be spent on getting there? How much should be allocated for the buying of souvenirs? Will a specialized wardrobe or equipment be needed for the vacation?

This can open up a wide variety of discussions in a family meeting of different kinds of value. What will the family be getting in return for its vacation dollar? Will there be more than one dimension to the trip? Will it be educational? Will you get to spend time with grandparents you don't see often?

▶ **Large purchases:** Getting the whole family involved in planning for, budgeting, and choosing a large purchase may seem like making more work for yourself, rather than less. On a certain level, it would be quicker and easier just to go out and buy the new refrigerator than to bring it up in a family meeting, discuss whether you really need it, delegate family members to research various brand names and price ranges, look into things like energy efficiency, decide which extras are worth paying for and which ones aren't, and come back to discuss it all.

And on a certain level, it's a whole lot easier for your boss to say, "Just show up for work at eight forty-five on Monday morning. I don't give a damn what you do about emergency child care. That's your responsibility." But we know that, in the long run, that philosophy is as bad for the company as it is for you. In the long run, it's better to take the extra

time and involve your whole family in these decisions. It's a great learning experience in family participation, in budgeting and money management
skills, in consumer education. Plus, you just might
wind up with a better refrigerator.

Positive experiences—such as family sharing
experiences, educational experiences, and financial
responsibility experiences—have a ripple effect.
They're likely to have positive consequences way beyond what you even foresee.

I want to make it clear, here, that I'm not saying every decision about a major purchase has to
be put to a democratic vote. That should be made
clear to the family from the start—you're asking
for their input and their involvement, but the final
decision will still be up to you, or to you and your
partner. Even so, it's possible to make it clear to
everyone in the family that their points of view are
valued.

▶ **Charities:** Families can and should research charities the way they research products. This should be
an important part of every family's sense of itself as
a family and its awareness of its place in, and its responsibility to, the community.

Bill Paying

If a family sits down and pays its bills together, and involves
the whole family in that project, it creates a real awareness
of how a family works, how money works, how real choices
are made.

Here's how I recommend doing this.

When you sit down together each month, have a computer finance management program, or an old-fashioned

ledger, set up to make the process as clear as possible. I suggest the following columns:

▶ **A column that shows the total amount of money available for paying bills.** This is your "money on hand," and it's obviously the place to start. You have to know what you have before you can know where you're going to allot it.

This is, as I mentioned, the part that's so hard for many parents, often simply because they're not used to doing it. Well, just bite the bullet and do it. If your financial situation is comfortable, and you're afraid that seeing that will make your kids want more, then this is an opportunity to discuss family responsibility and individual responsibility. You're sharing with your kids your family's entire philosophy of budgeting and goal setting, and you can expect them to understand.

If things are tight . . . well, I believe that it is good for kids to know and understand this. It's important to reassure your kids that you'll always work to keep a roof over their heads, to keep them fed and clothed, but that right now things are tough and you have to develop a budget to reflect the tough times.

▶ **A column in which all the bills are listed.** These are your regular monthly bills, the ones that come in and have to be paid. List each bill, and next to it leave room for two columns of figures: the total amount due for each bill, and the minimum amount due for each month.

For many of these, of course, the two figures will be the same. For others, such as credit card bills or your home mortgage, they'll be very different.

Explain to your kids how partial payment on a bill works—the whole concept of interest, and how you're actually paying a premium for the money, so that they understand what's at stake—what the difference is between making a partial payment and a full payment. You might not be able to make a full payment on every bill, but it's important that your kids realize you're not getting a bargain out of not making a full payment.

▶ **A column that lists all the items you spend money on each month.**

▶ **A column in which you'll put the amount of money you spend on each item.** You should have a very good idea of how much you're spending on each item.

      If you don't know where your money goes—and this is true for everyone in your household, make it your first priority to find out. You do this with a No Magic Money Log, which is a device that couldn't be simpler. You just take a notebook or a set of file cards—or your logbook for this project—and write down everything you spend. At the end of the month, you assign a category to each expenditure and then total up each category.

▶ **A column in which you'll put items for which you've set aside a medium-term savings budget line.** You've taught your kids how to do this, and you should be doing it, too.

▶ **A column for the dollar amounts you're putting aside for each item.**

▶ **A column for long-term savings:** your retirement, your kids' college fund.

▶ **A column for the dollar amounts you're putting aside for each of these items.**

Now it's time to sit down and start paying your bills . . . as a family. And your project here, as each child becomes old enough to participate in this task, is to teach her how to do it and to bring her into participating in the decision making that goes into making a budget.

Discuss with your child what comes first. Make sure he understands why you have to start with "money on hand" and figure out a bill-paying strategy based on that.

If there's enough money on hand to pay every bill you have, this part becomes very easy—and not as much of a lesson, actually. But if you have a mortgage or a car payment, that won't be the case.

More likely, though, decisions will have to be made. Give your child the first crack at making those decisions and explaining his reasons for them. Explain to him beforehand that you're the one who's going to be making the final decision. You don't want to put yourself in the position of leading a child to think that he's making the call, and then suddenly pulling rank and taking away that responsibility he thought he had. But you do want to include him in the decision-making process. As he grows older and gets more and more experienced with this sort of thing, he'll be able to make more and more responsible decisions in all aspects of his life.

Discuss with your child, as well, possible ways for adjusting the budget. Are there places the family can economize? Here again, it's important to explain to the child who's doing this for the first time that it takes some experience to be able to get a sense for these decisions. You might tell her that you'll make a note of her suggestions, but that you won't consider acting on them until she's been doing this for, say, six months. In the case of older children who have been part of the family bill-paying meetings for a while, you should be paying attention to their suggestions, even though they might not always be practical ("Let's get a hot tub so we can save money on individual showers").

The result of making this into a successful project? Your kids will become more responsible with money and feel more empowered as citizens of the household. You'll also, in a significant way, become a more responsible citizen of the household. By including your kids in family finance conferences, instead of giving them a vague "We can't afford it," you're creating a more open, healthy dialogue about money. You'll be honest when you say either "We can't afford it" or "That's not our top priority right now—this is."

Kids generally don't believe "We can't afford it." This is partly because they hear it too often, and they see other things being bought, and they don't have the big picture. It's also because kids don't really have a sense of how much money adults have, and they generally imagine it's more than it really is. This was brought home to me one day when I overheard a conversation, delivered absolutely seriously, between two eight-year-old boys on a New York City crosstown bus:

"I don't understand why they call him the Six-Million-Dollar Man. It can't have cost more than a million dollars for the parts to make him."

"Yes, but don't forget the scientists had to eat while they were making him."

Today, kids' concepts of how much people make comes from their exposure to the adults' salaries they do know about: salaries like Michael Jordan's.

Actually, it's not so hard to understand how they can get to feel that way. A friend of mine, who had never before played the state lottery, bought a ticket one day—and she won third prize. She was turning cartwheels. *If first prize is fifteen million dollars,* she figured, *I must have won at least ten thousand dollars.* She was brought down to earth abruptly by the thirty-dollar prize they handed her when she turned in her ticket. So how surprising it is to find your kids thinking, *I know my mom doesn't make anywhere near the ninety million dollars a year that Michael Jordan makes. She probably doesn't make more than half a million.*

Medium-Term Savings Purchases

You can define medium-term savings the way you define it for your kids: as anything that you can't pay for out of cash on hand (like your annual vacation, or tickets to take the whole family to see *The Lion King*), although most medium-term savings goals are items you'll figure on being able to afford in five to ten years. A vacation cottage is a medium-term savings goal. So are predictable expenses like that remodeling job you want to do on your kitchen.

There are some medium-term savings projects that are yours alone. You have a right to that new guitar or that mountain bike if you can budget for it—you work hard for your money. Also, since medium-term projects can include those that require a substantial amount of money and perhaps as much as eight to ten years of planning time, there are many that will be your decision alone, or yours and your partner's.

But anything that's a family benefit can be a family project. The whole family can discuss a vacation or a new car. They can get together and discuss larger things, too, like whether that longer-medium-term project, the one that will involve a serious commitment to saving, should be a boat, a cottage in the country, or perhaps a six-month sabbatical for mom so that the family can live abroad and study.

Here's what goes into the discussion of a family project that involves budgetary decisions:

- ▶ **What do you want?** This can be the subject of a family meeting, and anyone in the family can call a family meeting to present a proposal.
- ▶ **What are the benefits to the family?** The person who makes the proposal is responsible for convincing the family that it's something they should go for.

Something can be of benefit to the family for any number of reasons, and one of them might be the happiness or enrichment of one member of the family: "I want to propose that the family send me to soccer camp this summer. It'll cost a thousand dollars, but I have two hundred dollars saved and I'll work and pay three hundred dollars more into the family fund by the end of the year. I think that the family can afford five hundred dollars for special enrichment projects for each of us, and I'd like this to be mine."

▶ **What will it cost?** The person who's bringing the proposal should have done some research before she gets to the meeting. Is it the best price? If it involves an expenditure that's more than the family can afford right now, what's the best way to pay for it? Is it something that can be saved up for? Is it something that should be bought on some kind of payment plan—and if so, what is the real cost?

▶ **What are alternate suggestions?** What other ways can this part of the family budget be used, and which is the best way?

▶ **If the family agrees in principle on this idea, is this the best proposal?** Is there a better value? Should the family appoint a committee to do more research?

▶ **Who ultimately decides?** You need to let the family know in advance how the decision will be made. Sometimes it can be "majority rules"; other times, you'll take the family's input under advisement but reserve the right to make your own decision.

Don't forget, these budgetary decisions are good training ground for the younger citizens of your family, too. They might not be able to contribute much in the way of sophisticated research into what kind of new car you should get. But they can make presentations on what kind of breakfast cereal the family should be eating. They can report on the cost-nutrition value ratio of some of the foods you buy at the supermarket. Don't laugh. The words might be big, but it's a concept that little children can handle.

Charities

Everything that's true about how families can meet and decide together what they want to get is equally true here. Families can get together and decide what they want to give. These decisions are just as important, and they should be researched and discussed in the same way.

Sometimes a family will decide to adopt one charity and then make the donation in the name of the family. Other times, everyone will have different charities. Either way, the discussion makes for wonderful family sharing.

In the first case, someone (often the youngest child) can be delegated to report on how the family charity fund is doing and what activities and successes the family charity has achieved.

In the latter, the reports can be individual. That's the way it is in my family. Rhett cares deeply about animals and the environment. His charities are the World Wildlife Federation and saving the rain forest—he's contributed to a fund that buys up rain forest acreage so it will remain forever wild. Kyle's interest is in people. She got interested in UNICEF as a little girl trick-or-treating for UNICEF, and now she's a youth ambassador for that wonderful organization.

Remember that giving back to the community, and making a difference in the lives of those less fortunate than you are, can be done with time and effort as well as with money. These exercises of charity are just as valuable, and they can be proposed and discussed in the same way that financial gifts can be.

In the same way, there are nonfinancial things a family can do *for* itself, also, and these things can be proposed and discussed in family meetings: a current events discussion one evening at dinner, a family fitness program, a regular evening of reading aloud if the children are younger, or discussing a book everyone's read if they're older.

Chapter 13

Holiday Projects

T hings that happen only once a year certainly ought to qualify as projects, but too often they turn into processes. They come up on us before we know it, they sweep us up in confusion and chaos, and before we know it they're over, and we make vague vows that we're certainly not going to do it that way again next year. But unless we stop and think about it, and plan, we will be doing it exactly that way again next year.

Holidays happen every year—family holidays, national holidays, religious holidays. There are unfathomable holidays—if your husband and sons have twenty guys over every January to watch the Super Bowl, that's a holiday. In fact, in the 1990s, Super Bowl Sunday has become the second-biggest holiday in America in terms of parties and celebrations after Thanksgiving.

What Do You Celebrate, and How?

Here's a family issue that's also a corporate issue, and once again, your experience in the corporate world can reflect back to your strategy as family CEO. All major corporations have event planners. Events, and how they're handled, are an important reflection of the corporation.

How many days of the year are predictably out of the ordinary for you because they involve spending money, entertaining a group of people, buying presents, or performing rituals? Let's start with those.

Fill out the checklist on pages 162 to 167. Check off each item you celebrate by doing something special, and for those items you've checked, fill out the rest of the checklist. If you both love something and dread it, check both. Do the last category, the amount of money you spend on the holiday, like this:

- ▶ **If you know for certain how much you budget for and spend on a holiday, put down the figure.**
- ▶ **If you can make a pretty good estimate, put down that figure with a question mark.**
- ▶ **If you have no idea how much you spend, put in a question mark (for now).** Don't be surprised if there's a strong correlation between the "dread it" holidays and the question mark holidays.

Holiday

Kid's birthday

We celebrate (yes/no):
- ▶ Love it
- ▶ Dread it
- ▶ Generally under control

▶ Generally out of control
▶ $ spent

Mom's birthday

We celebrate (yes/no):
▶ Love it
▶ Dread it
▶ Generally under control
▶ Generally out of control
▶ $ spent

Dad's birthday

We celebrate (yes/no):
▶ Love it
▶ Dread it
▶ Generally under control
▶ Generally out of control
▶ $ spent

Grandparents' birthdays

We celebrate (yes/no):
▶ Love it
▶ Dread it
▶ Generally under control
▶ Generally out of control
▶ $ spent

Other relatives' birthdays

We celebrate (yes/no):
▶ Love it
▶ Dread it
▶ Generally under control
▶ Generally out of control
▶ $ spent

Wedding anniversary

We celebrate (yes/no):
▶ Love it
▶ Dread it
▶ Generally under control
▶ Generally out of control
▶ $ spent

Family reunion

We celebrate (yes/no):
▶ Love it
▶ Dread it
▶ Generally under control
▶ Generally out of control
▶ $ spent

Other (fill in)

We celebrate (yes/no):
▶ Love it
▶ Dread it
▶ Generally under control
▶ Generally out of control
▶ $ spent

Rather than unintentionally offending anyone by leaving anything out, or raising questions about the order I might place these in, I'll leave this next checklist for you to fill in. You know your individual faith better than I do, and what holidays you celebrate in honor of your religion.

Religious Holidays

Holiday (fill in)

We celebrate (yes/no):
▶ Love it
▶ Dread it

► Generally under control
► Generally out of control
► $ spent

National holidays are those celebrations that we share in common with large numbers of our fellow citizens: Thanksgiving, a Super Bowl party, or a big Labor Day picnic. For the sake of stirring your minds to think about this, I've included several of the major American holidays, but this process, of course, can apply equally well to holidays in other national traditions.

National Holidays

Thanksgiving

We celebrate (yes/no):
► Love it
► Dread it
► Generally under control
► Generally out of control
► $ spent

Fourth of July

We celebrate (yes/no):
► Love it
► Dread it
► Generally under control
► Generally out of control
► $ spent

Labor Day

We celebrate (yes/no):
► Love it
► Dread it
► Generally under control

▶ Generally out of control
▶ $ spent

Mother's Day

We celebrate (yes/no):
▶ Love it
▶ Dread it
▶ Generally under control
▶ Generally out of control
▶ $ spent

Father's Day

We celebrate (yes/no):
▶ Love it
▶ Dread it
▶ Generally under control
▶ Generally out of control
▶ $ spent

Valentine's Day

We celebrate (yes/no):
▶ Love it
▶ Dread it
▶ Generally under control
▶ Generally out of control
▶ $ spent

Super Bowl Sunday

We celebrate (yes/no):
▶ Love it
▶ Dread it
▶ Generally under control
▶ Generally out of control
▶ $ spent

Halloween
▶ We celebrate (yes/no):
▶ Love it
▶ Dread it
▶ Generally under control
▶ Generally out of control
▶ $ spent

Fixing What's Broke

We all know that "If it ain't broke, don't fix it" is not a perfect formula. We do sometimes have to fix things that don't appear to be broken.

But it's only common sense to fix the things that are broken first. So, start by paying attention to holidays you've marked "Dread it" and go from there to the "Love it but dread it."

Make *absolutely sure* that you give prompt attention to the holidays that have a question mark in the budget category.

Here are the main reasons women with families have told me they dread holidays:

▶ Too expensive
▶ Too chaotic
▶ Too exhausting
▶ "I have to do everything"
▶ Spirit of holiday is lost

That Holiday Spirit

If you feel that the spirit of a holiday has been lost, then it probably has been. And if it has been lost, then everyone feels it, whether they know it or not. It's possible for gift-giving holidays like birthdays and Christmas to degenerate into joyless orgies of gift unwrapping—grim, breathless affairs that invariably seem to end with huge trash cans full of ripped boxes and lacerated wrapping paper, blank stares that seem to say "Is that all?" and moods that seem to flare suddenly into fights or tantrums.

Everyone feels it, but everyone doesn't always recognize the feelings. Getting stuff can be a drug, and like any other drug, it's addictive, it makes the addict want more and more, it starts giving less and less pleasure, and the addict can't imagine being without it. Kids can start looking at it as life's report card for them—how much they get is a measure of their worth.

I've appeared on national TV to counsel some families who literally could not stop spending money on their kids. They had run up enormous debts, and they were in danger of defaulting on their mortgages. Their kids had so much expensive junk, from Barbie accessories to sports equipment to expensive electronics to new wings built on the house to hold all their stuff (no, I'm not making this last item up), that other kids in the TV studio audience weren't listening with envy, they were cringing with embarrassed disbelief. On TV, the kids said yes, they liked having all this stuff, and yes, they expected it, and yes, they expected their parents to outdo themselves yet again this year at Christmas. But their eyes were hollow and empty. They were overstimulated to the point that they seemed very nearly incapable of joy.

When I sat down and worked with these families on creating a budget, the kids protested at first. They said that they weren't interested in all this boring stuff and that they liked things the way they were. But that facade didn't hold up. Underneath—and not all that far underneath—they knew that things weren't right and that they were missing something. They were missing a sense of themselves, a sense of family closeness, and the sense of self-worth that responsibility brings.

I wasn't surprised that I was able to work with these families who seemed so far gone down the road of financial dysfunctionality. This is what I do, and you're best off going into a project with confidence. But I was a little surprised at how quickly the transformation happened, how close under the surface that yearning for responsibility and stability really was.

If it's there in families that were so far out over the edge, it's probably there for your family, too.

Open up a discussion at a family meeting. What are our family priorities? Which means more to everyone in the family—making sure that all the silver is polished the week before Thanksgiving or being together? Having two kinds of potatoes, three kinds of stuffing, and four different flavors of homemade pies or being together? Buying new wardrobes to impress relatives or being together? To the question Why can't we have both? or Why can't we have them all? you can answer with a breakdown of the amount of woman-hours involved with bringing about each one of those things. It doesn't have to be a martyr thing, just a cost-benefit analysis.

This can lead to a talk about the real spirit of the holidays. Once everyone is on the same wavelength of wanting to find that spirit, everyone will have something to add. Making the holidays a positive experience for everyone becomes a family project, one that addresses a specific problem, one for which you can plot a strategy and assign personnel and resources, and one that you can analyze when it's over.

At Alison's family meeting, they had just about concluded a discussion on their new approach to the holidays. They had decided that their goals were to have the family together and to make sure to invite a couple of people who would otherwise be alone. They'd all agreed that they didn't need to go into debt, and they'd set a gift limit of twenty dollars apiece for gifts within the family. Then Whitney said, "You know, there's just one thing. Are we going to tell Grandma in advance or just sort of, like, spring the paper plates and the mashed potatoes from Boston Market on her as a surprise?"

Whitney was looking accusatory. Alison was ready to get defensive, but she stopped herself. At another time, she might have snapped back at Whitney. But this was a family meeting. It was for airing and sharing.

"Thank you, honey," she said. "You know, I really hadn't taken that into account. Of course we have to tell her."

Whitney grinned a little. "I'll volunteer to do it," she said. "I think I can do a better job of it. After all, I know how hard it is for mothers and daughters to communicate sometimes."

"And sometimes daughters are the greatest people in the world," Alison told her. "Thank you, honey. I'll delegate the responsibility to you with great appreciation."

Expensive, Chaotic, Exhausting

We can't promise that holidays won't be a little exhausting. Any large project is going to take something out of you. The goal here is a positive balance sheet. You want to end up, after the holidays, sitting back and sipping a cup of herbal tea, taking a deep breath, and saying "Wow, that was great!" not "I never want to go through that again."

You want the effort to be worth it.

It's worth it if it's not too expensive, so that you don't end up feeling as though you paid for a lot more than what you got in return and wondering how on earth you're going to dig yourself out of the financial hole you've just gotten yourself into.

It's worth it if it's not too chaotic, so that you can see tangible results for all the energy you spent. When Hollywood producers spend $80 million on a movie, they always say that they like to "see the money up there on the screen"—they want that money to have gone for audience-attracting stars, striking and beautiful locations, great stunts, and great special effects. They don't want to have paid a crew for two weeks when the scene could have been shot in three days if things had been better organized. And *you* don't want to find yourself sitting down with that cup of tea, gazing around at a monstrous mess, and realizing that a large part of the reason why you're exhausted is that you've been running around in circles, duplicating a lot of effort, and generally wasting time.

Budgets

There are two methods of figuring out a holiday budget, and ultimately you're going to have to use both of them.

One of them is to do a No Magic Holiday Log. Figure out, as best you can, everything you've spent on recent holidays. Then, do an actual No Magic Holiday Log for upcoming holidays in which you keep a thorough log of everything you do spend.

Unfortunately, there are two flaws to this method. First, you need to get going right away; you don't want to wait through another holiday in which you don't alter your spending patterns so that you can keep a No Magic Holiday Log (the estimated one will *always* be lower than what you really spend). Second, if you start out with what you're actually spending and try to figure out what you can cut down, you won't cut down enough. Holidays are like that. Guilt or generosity always gets the better of us, and we end up saying, "Oh, I can't do without *that* . . ."

The first thing to do is to look at your total budget and

decide on a realistic figure that you can afford to spend on the holiday without going into debt.

Then do the No Magic Holiday Estimated Log, figure out what you guess you're spending, and start cutting back. And don't stop cutting until you reach the figure you can afford.

Suppose that cuts seriously into the "Oh, I can't do without *that . . .*" items. Will that ruin your holiday?

No. You know, not only intellectually but in your heart, that it's not money that makes a holiday. It's not three kinds of stuffing that makes a holiday. It's not more expensive gifts than last year that makes a holiday. It's not buying a new linen tablecloth that makes a holiday.

Project Manager: Danielle Ormby, twenty-nine, department store manager. Married, mom of Steve, eight; Eric, six; and Annalee, three.

I have two really different models for how to plan a holiday. One— the one that I've always used in the past—is my grandmother. That's the formal model. My grandmother's table for a holiday meal could have been photographed and used as a centerfold for *House Beautiful.* And believe me, she prepared for it as though a photographer were going to come calling.

Every year, since I was a little girl, I would go over to her house before Thanksgiving and Christmas. We'd polish the silver. We'd bake cookies from scratch and decorate them just so with a little glitter dust. We'd clean like crazy. When I was little—seven or eight or nine years old—I felt like I was part of something really important, and I was incredibly honored to be allowed to do my share. But I was always afraid that I'd do something wrong and ruin it for Grandma, and it would be all my fault.

Now we still do Thanksgiving at Grandma's, and my mother and my sister and I do a lot more of the work. We never quite do it right, and Grandma lets us know about it, believe me. It's not the most fun in the world to do those Thanksgivings, but we do them out of love and respect, and I can tell you that we do the best we darn well can to make them perfect!

Here's my other model, and I know you'll think this is dumb. Even *I* think it's dumb. In fact, I think it's Dumb and Dumber. But here goes . . .

I went over to my brother's this year for Super Bowl Sunday with my husband Steve, and Steve Junior, and Eric.

My brother Tom has an apartment that's sort of like *The Odd Couple* if Felix had thrown up his hands in disgust and moved out. He ordered in a bunch of pizzas, had some beer and soft drinks, chips and dips right out of the container. There were some hot dogs in the kitchen next to the microwave, and anyone who wanted to could nuke one up.

I was totally appalled. My sons thought they'd gone to heaven.

After I overcame my initial impulse to run screaming out of the room, I started to notice something. Everyone was having a great time.

I started to feel like an anthropologist studying some strange and unfamiliar tribal culture.

For example, I asked one of Tom's friends, if this game was such a great big deal, why were they turning down the sound to listen to a rap song? "The Super Bowl is always the most boring game of the year," he said. "It's a monstrous anticlimax."

This made a lot of sense. Yeah, right. If I knew I was going to be watching the most boring game of the year, I'd go out shopping instead of watching it.

In fact, I did go out shopping after the first half was over, when I saw that the boys were going to be fine. When they came home with their father, they were still raving about what a great time they'd had.

We had a family meeting. We talked about the things that everyone loved, and we talked about the things that we just did because we did them. We ended up with our own kind of holiday, which combines the best of Grandma's traditionalism and Tommy's informality into a new tradition that is really our own. And we're a lot happier.

The point is, talk these things out. Don't assume that it has to be a certain way, and don't assume that you know what everyone wants. Ask people what they want. Have a family meeting. And you can have more than one. People change, especially kids. Even family traditions don't have to be etched in stone.

The No Magic Holiday Log

Make sure, as you make out this log, that you remember to account for all the expenses you'll incur that are specific to the holiday—that is, expenses that you wouldn't have if it weren't for the holiday.

Include all of these:

- ▶ **Gifts**
- ▶ **Food for entertaining**
- ▶ **Cleaning (supplies and help) for the holiday**
- ▶ **Cleaning (supplies and help) after the holiday**
- ▶ **Clothing and accessories bought for the holiday**
- ▶ **Special laundry and dry cleaning expenses for the holiday**
- ▶ **Decorating for the holiday:** This includes any expenses for items that are absolutely holiday-specific, from Christmas lights to menorahs to red-white-and-blue bunting for a Fourth of July picnic to inexpensive birthday tablecloths and napkins with pictures of clowns on them to personalized tablecloths and napkins with the birthday child's name and age on them.
- ▶ **Rentals (space):** This includes the rental of a hall or a rec field, an arcade, or a mansion—any space for a party or celebration that's outside your home.
- ▶ **Rentals (equipment):** This includes anything from a doughnut maker to a helium tank for balloons.

► **Entertainment:** Do you hire a band for your annual Christmas party? Get balloons or pony rides for a kid's party? Take a group to a sports event as part of a celebration?

► **Transportation:** This includes the cost of bringing relatives or friends in from out of town, if your family is paying for it (and putting them up in a motel or bed-and-breakfast, if your family is paying for that). It also includes any unusual driving you have to do and any unusual parking expenses you have to incur in holiday shopping.

► **Utilities:** If your electric bill goes up every December because you love to decorate your house and yard with Christmas lights, then this is a holiday expense that must be entered.

► **Phone and postage:** Any big celebration that involves a lot of people, especially one that involves people who live out of town, might include these expenses. Any celebration that involves gifts might include the mailing of packages. If you send Christmas cards, they have to be bought (or made, if you have a family picture put on them).

► **Gratuities:** Are you expected to tip your doorkeeper at Christmas? Your refuse-removal service person? Your package-delivery service person?

► **Last-minute gift expenses:** This needs to be a category separate from the gifts you know about. What if your brother suddenly shows up for Christmas with a new girlfriend?

► **Interest** on any credit charges you might have accumulated over the holidays.

If you start going over your budget, start cutting back. You knew, before you started this project, that there would be items you hadn't thought of when you made your estimated No Magic Holiday Log.

If you don't absolutely succeed in keeping to your budget the first time you do this, don't beat up on yourself for it. Gather the whole team together for a project review. What did you do well? What can you do better? What methods or steps can you take to improve your performance?

This is where an actual No Magic Holiday Log will be invaluable to you. So make sure that you keep one!

Time Budgeting

The most effective steps in cutting down chaos and duplication in any project are:

▶ Identify tasks.
▶ Assign tasks.
▶ Set up a timetable.

In the case of a holiday project, a good first step might be a brainstorming session on the general subject of *What are we not going to do this year?*

Brainstorming is often a good idea at the inception of a project. It means you just toss out ideas off the top of your head, with no holds barred, no sacred cows—anyone is allowed to say anything.

If you start with what shouldn't be done, who knows what you'll find that can be jettisoned? Maybe now that the kids are older, they think all those Christmas lawn decorations that you've been putting up every year, which they loved when they were six, are a little bit corny now. That'll save a couple of evenings of labor, some money on utilities, and the money you normally set aside to buy a new lawn piece each year. You might even have a yard sale, get rid of the ones you have, and make a few dollars that you can add to the holiday budget.

When you identify what's generally agreed upon as un-
necessary—and this list might be longer than you think—
you've made an important first step, and one that you can
build on. If you've eliminated the stuff that no one thinks is
important, what you have left is bound to be stuff that people do care about—which is, from any manager's point of
view, an excellent place to start.

Now, the tasks you're identifying are going to be tasks
for which there's some enthusiasm, which means that you'll
be assigning those tasks to people who want to see that
they're carried out.

Charity and Holidays

For us, a family project around Thanksgiving and Hanukkah
has always been volunteering some time to work with the
homeless.

I've said before how important I believe it is to share
what we have—and our time is our most important possession—with those less fortunate than we are. I've talked about
the fourth jar in the four-jar system, the one for charity. I've
talked about charitable donations being an important part of
every family budget plan. Well, this is equally true of service, of sharing your time.

This does not have to be something exclusive to the
holiday season. There is always work to be done, from ongoing projects like literacy volunteering to special projects
like helping to rebuild a vandalized church. But the holidays
are a special time for realizing the importance of family.
They're a special time for realizing how blessed we are to
have homes and families, and for reaching out to share
our blessedness with others.

You can look to business as a model here, too. Tim
Schwertzfeger, CEO of the Chicago financial service firm Nu-

veen, Inc., noticed that the firm's annual summer picnic, a tradition for generations, had become more of an ordeal than a treat for most employees. He proposed replacing it with a series of Volunteer Days, in which the firm's employees would turn out as a team to build a playground in an inner-city neighborhood. He got the most enthusiastic response he had ever gotten to a suggestion, and he found that the Volunteer Days did the job that the company picnic was supposed to but didn't: raising morale and bringing people together.

Chapter 14

Future Projects

The big future projects are these:

- ▶ **Buying a house** (if you don't have one already)
- ▶ **Kids' college fund**
- ▶ **Retirement**

Everything else is secondary, so let's start with these. And in general, I recommend that for the items in this chapter, major items that involve long-term planning and long-term saving, the project team be you, or you and your partner.

Buying a house is, generally, a medium-term savings goal, something that you're probably considering within five to ten years in the future (if you're planning something closer than that, then I'll assume that you've mostly done your saving already and that you have your down payment or the greater part of it).

Kids' college expenses, if your kids are young, will be a long-term expense, and so will retirement.

In order to budget for these things, you need to have a sense of how much you'll need to have in the future and how much you'll need to save, on a regular basis, to get there. For long-term savings, and even for the longer-medium-term savings, you can count on your money making money for you, if you invest it. I'll include a table at the end of this chapter that will tell you how to figure out the rate of return on various long-term investments, but here's a thumbnail guide: the Rule of 72. The rate of return on your investment, divided into 72, equals the number of years it will take your investment to double. An investment at 9 percent will double in eight years, then double again in another eight years, and so on.

You can use a chart like this:

Long-Term Savings Goals

Goal	$ needed	Target date	Savings needed (per year)

To figure out how your medium-term savings goals fit into your budget, you can calculate either by month or by year, like this:

Medium-Term Savings Goals

Goal	$ needed	Target date	Savings needed (per month)	(per year)

The savings you need for your children's college, and the savings for your retirement, should be your major concerns. They each should account for between 40 and 45 percent of your savings goals.

One-of-a-Kind Projects

The projects you build around one-of-a-kind events are similar to holiday projects in the kind of planning that you have to do—food, entertaining, gifts, putting people up, renting space—but they have their own special nature, too. I'm talking about events like the following:

► Weddings
► Engagements
► Bridal showers
► Parents' golden wedding anniversaries
► Bar/Bas Mitzvahs
► Christenings
► First communions
► Sweet sixteens
► College graduations
► High school graduations
► Senior proms
► Funerals

These are just a few examples. Different families have different one-of-a-kind occasions, and mark them in different ways. The point here is, there are predictable events in your family's future that will be marked by some sort of ceremony, and those ceremonies will cost money.

Some of them are more precisely predictable than others. You know exactly when your daughter is going to turn sixteen; you don't know exactly when she's going to get married. But this is the least important factor in long-range planning. A ballpark estimate of when an event is going to happen is just fine. After all, the biggest event that you need to save for is your retirement, and you have only a general idea of when that will happen.

First Steps in Planning

When you're planning for the future—either the medium-term (the next five to ten years) or the long-term future—it never hurts to start out by thinking big, with a wish list.

Start by writing down a list of every one-of-a-kind event you can imagine yourself celebrating or commemorating. First, all you need is the list. And don't forget, by the way, that any list you make up for predictable future events must also include a category for unpredictable future events.

Next, start figuring out how important each of these events are going to be. Use the following scale:

1. This isn't something we would make an occasion of.
2. We would make an occasion of this, but it wouldn't be a big ceremony.
3. If we could afford it, we'd make a major occasion of this.
4. This *is* a major ceremonial occasion in our family, and we'll do whatever it takes to make sure it happens.

For each item you've marked as a 4, it's time to start figuring out how you're going to get there.

There's one rule I believe in very strongly for all these one-of-a-kind occasions. If they're important to you, they should be important enough to plan in advance and save up for. You should never go into debt for them.

So do whatever research you need to do to find out how much the event will cost. This isn't always easy, and at best involves estimated figures. This is all right. It's understood that when you're planning for some distance in the future, you know that things can change. None of these figures should be written in stone. Your priorities might change; your financial circumstances might change.

Still, how do you research the cost of an event in the future? Prices don't stay the same for anything.

Here's a rough guideline—close enough for your purposes in doing this sort of planning: increase the price by 50 percent for events that will take place five to seven years in the future; double the price for events that will take place eight to twelve years in the future; triple the price for events thirteen to seventeen years in the future; and quadruple the price for events seventeen to twenty-two years in the future.

Then you can use a chart like the one below:

Event:
Years in future:

Item	Cost	Estimated cost at time of event
Catering		
for ____ people		
for ____ people		
for ____ people		
Flowers		
Music		
Photographer		
Transportation		
Gift		
Location		
Cost of ceremony		
Other		
Total		

What If . . . ?

What if your child decides to pass on the big wedding you have planned for her? Does all that saving go to waste?

Of course not. There are plenty of ways of handling

that sum of money you've put aside. One is: "Hey, great—more popcorn for the rest of us!" That isn't so hard-hearted as it sounds. Discuss it with your child (your adult child, at this point). Maybe she'll say, "Sure, I'm not much on ceremony—let's take that money and put it toward Grandma and Grandpa's around-the-world cruise for their fiftieth anniversary."

The other is: Give it to your child anyway, as part of a down payment on a new home or to furnish an apartment.

Or don't make specific plans. The advantage of making specific plans (which can always be changed) is that you're more apt to find some way to save for something you've planned for specifically. But it's also possible to put a certain amount into savings/investment for each child, figuring that you and your kids can decide later on how it will be used.

Ultimately, if this is money that you've saved, the decision should be yours. Compare the following statements:

"Mom, I really want a horse. I'm not ever going to want to go to some yucky old senior prom. We can take that money and put it toward getting a horse." (If it's practical in other ways, why not?)

"Mom, I really want a horse. I'm not ever going to get married, so I don't have to worry about saving up for a fancy wedding. We can take that money and put it toward getting a horse." (She very likely will get married someday. But maybe she really will, even then, prefer the horse to a big wedding. You know your daughter. You can make an intelligent judgment about how much the horse means to her now and how much the wedding is likely to mean to her later. You can talk to her about how much of her own money she can spend on a horse. But you'll give it some thought before you make a decision.)

"Mom, I really want a horse. I'm going to be a horse breeder when I grow up—I'm not ever going to have to go to college. We can take my college money and get a horse with it." (Uh-uh. You don't even have to think about this one twice.)

What, on the other hand, if your child wants more than you've budgeted? Sometimes excitement can take over when you're dealing with a one-of-a-kind event. I was faced with this problem when I counseled a family on the Oprah Winfrey show. The family (we'll call them the Wilsons) had a serious spending problem anyway, which is what had brought them to Oprah, and to me. They didn't know how to budget, and they didn't know how to stop spending money.

Their daughter's wedding had precipitated a real crisis. If they didn't hold the line on spending here, they'd be on a collision course with bankruptcy.

But a wedding is special. If you're accustomed to thinking that special equals spending, and the more special, the more spending, it's hard to make that the first step in an austerity program.

Wanda, the daughter, had the same answer to everything.

"It's my *wedding*!" was her entire argument, and since that really isn't an argument, there was no answer to it. The parents asked me, wistfully, "Couldn't we start economizing *after* the wedding?"

But they knew that was impossible. And it never works, anyway. Once you start making exceptions every exception becomes the one that you absolutely can't draw the line on. Then making an exception is no longer an exception; it's your way of life. It was already a way of life for the Wilsons.

Wanda had started by buying a $1,000 dress. And since she had the dress, she had to have the shoes to go with it, she had to have everything else that lived up to the standard of that dress.

I talked to Wanda's parents. We went over their books carefully and figured out that they could actually afford a total of $5,000 for this wedding. Armed with those figures, I sat down with Wanda. Her parents had presented her with vague fears; they had countered her "It's my *wedding!*" with "But dear, I don't know how we're going to come up with the money." That didn't mean anything to Wanda, because her parents had always said it, and they'd always come up with the money somewhere.

Wanda had never actually seen her parent's balance sheet before. She didn't know how much they made. She didn't know how much they owed. She had never had to compare the cost of her wedding to any other standard except how much she wanted it.

It wasn't easy for her. Her first response was resentment, a resentment that echoed her parents' wistful "Couldn't we start economizing later?" Her angry response was, "Why couldn't I have found about this later?" That went along with "Why couldn't they have started economizing earlier, so they'd have more money for my wedding?" But she knew that most of the Wilsons' expenses had always been for her and her brother and sister.

The resentment gave way, slowly, to realism, and I knew I had gotten through to her when she said, hesitantly:

"Well . . . I know where I can get a pair of shoes wholesale . . . for thirty-five dollars."

I could see the look in her eyes. It's the one that I always watch for . . . the first realization that real empowerment doesn't come from deciding, blindly, that you can spend whatever you want. It comes from knowing you control your spending, it doesn't control you.

We started researching costs, and by the time we were done, we had put together a $5,000 wedding that Wanda was proud of. It didn't feel tacky or cut-rate to her; it felt like a triumph.

If you have a family that's already money-responsible—which means a family that shares responsibility and understanding in budgeting matters—then this becomes a simple equation. You know what you can put in, from the family budget, to a prom or a sweet sixteen or even a wedding. If your child wants something more elaborate, she can pay for it herself.

This is the same principle you can use for regular expenses, too. If the difference between the good quality sneakers your child needs for school and the Air Jordans he wants is $75, he can have the Air Jordans if he pays the extra $75.

Elective Medical Expenses

You can't predict what your medical expenses are going to be over a lifetime, which is why you have medical insurance. But there are certain elective medical/dental expenses that might run in your family. If you had braces, or a nose job, there's a good chance your kids might need the same things. Check to see if your insurance policy pays for these things, or pays for part of them.

Windfalls

Sometimes you'll get money that you weren't expecting.

I don't mean winning the lottery. Very few readers of this book are ever going to have to deal with that eventuality. In fact, as someone who believes in a carefully planned investment strategy, I don't even recommend that you play it. But there are other kinds of windfalls.

At certain times in your life, you might well come into the possession of sums of money—even large sums—that are over and above what you're budgeting with. An inheritance is one of the most common. Or perhaps an unexpected, un-budgeted-for bonus. What do you with this extra money?

Well, here's my advice, and it's simple:

Put 40 to 45 percent into your kids' college fund.

Put 40 to 45 percent into your retirement fund.

Put the rest into your fund for one-of-a-kind expenses.

Learning Projects

'Ve always made the point, in my books and lectures, and in workshops I've done with parents around the country, that teaching financial responsibility is a crucial step in teaching responsibility of all sorts. Money is a tool, a medium of exchange. It represents, symbolically, all the possible varieties of social exchange. You can get it, spend it, save it, or share it. It represents, when handled properly, an absolutely fair exchange.

Of course, it can be an ingredient in severely unfair exchanges, too, which is why it's important for us to teach our kids to recognize the difference. That's why I recommend all those exercises: shopping games we teach our littlest ones, in which they learn how to make change and to understand the values of different denominations of coins and bills; the value-recognizing games, where they learn to go through a supermarket and figure out the best buys on the most nutritious food.

It's why I recommend that we include our kids in family bill paying and budget making. The more they know about how things work financially, the more they understand fairness, the more they know that they're being treated fairly, and the more they know that the transactions they make—the getting, spending, saving, and sharing of their own money—are part of a larger system that makes sense, and also runs according to rules.

As a guest expert on the Oprah Winfrey show, I worked with several families who didn't know how to stop spending, including families who didn't know how to stop spending on their children. The kids in those families had new bikes, stereos, computers, and home entertainment centers—the parents just kept spending more and more on them. The kids had everything they could ever want, but they weren't happy. They kept wanting more, kept asking for more, and their parents kept going deeper into debt to give them more.

These families were there to be helped and to spark a serious discussion of these issues. Nevertheless, there was a lot of hostility from the audience toward the families, who were seen as irresponsible, and toward the kids, who were seen as selfish, ungrateful little beasts. Even the other kids in the audience didn't envy these children all the stuff they were getting.

And the kids, being kids, got hostile in return, and sassed back at the audience, saying they did too think they deserved all that stuff they were getting, and they wanted more, a lot more, and their parents darn well better be getting it for them.

But they didn't mean it. They were out of balance, and they knew they were out of balance. That awareness was not even buried very deep under the surface, either—I was able to tap it remarkably quickly when I sat down and included them in a discussion of the family budget.

It was the inclusion that made the difference. That and

the fairness. The kids had gotten spoiled, it's true; and yes, it was the fault of the parents.

It happens. People—even parents—make mistakes, and sometimes they're bad mistakes. As mistakes go, there are a lot worse than these, including abuse and abandonment, but these are still mistakes that have to be taken seriously.

The parents had tried to turn this situation around in the past, but their attempts had been halfhearted and had never made any difference. They'd told the kids, "We've got to start cutting down on expenses. Money doesn't grow on trees, you know." But they didn't know. They actually had seen no evidence to prove to them that money didn't grow on trees. Their parents had said they couldn't afford the TV, but then they went ahead and bought it. They'd said they couldn't afford the computer, but then they went ahead and bought it. Saying that they couldn't afford something was, apparently, something that parents did before they went out and bought you stuff.

This was what they'd learned; these were the messages they'd been sent. Sure, they could have looked around at other kids whose parents did roughly the same kind of work that their parents did. They could have noticed that those kids didn't seem to have nearly as much stuff as they did.

But that didn't happen, either, and there wasn't any point in my pointing fingers and blaming anyone. My job was to find an answer, and the best answer I could find, for kids and parents alike, was making them part of the team. The parents hadn't meant to be bad parents—they were trying to be good, to give their children things they'd never had, and to shelter them from the harsh realities of the world.

But those realities had become nowhere near as harsh as the fantasy that kids and parents both had been trapped in, and trapped separately.

I decided to make the kids a part of the team and empower them with knowledge of the whole picture. I showed them where the money went. I showed them how credit card debt worked and how much it cost to pay for spending money you didn't actually have. I showed them the relationship between things bought and hours worked. I demonstrated the problem to them, and I gave them responsibility for being part of the team that worked out the solution to the problem.

It was a strategy that worked, and I continue to believe it's the best strategy. We've learned, in business, that a project-oriented approach is the best way to increase productivity, to encourage loyalty, and to foster a working spirit that strengthens the individual as well as helping the company.

We've learned, in those businesses that have been responsive to women and to families, that the more inclusive this team-oriented approach is, the better the results are. The businesses that have expanded their team approach to include backup child care, family-friendly offices, and awareness of the education and enrichment goals of families, have flourished.

We can take a lot of these lessons back home with us. A team approach at home has to be inclusive, too. We can't shield our kids from responsibility in some areas and expect them to be responsible in others. Kids believe in fairness, and they understand it when they see it.

There's one more lesson that we can take home with us from work. Problems are to be solved. There is nothing—*nothing*—to be gained from *not* solving a problem. There are no *Gotcha!*s at work. There's never an advantage to saying, "Well, we didn't meet that deadline, and it was Joe's fault." The advantage is in saying, "We met the deadline, and it was a team effort, and Joe did a great job." If we had to rally behind Joe when we had doubts about him—if we weren't always sure we *liked* Joe—none of those things matter in comparison to the personal satisfaction, the job satisfaction,

and the advancement of the business that come from meeting the deadline.

If these things are true in the workplace, they're even
more true at home.

The fairness that you set up and achieve in using
money—work for pay, the jar system, family meetings to discuss family expenses like charities, holidays, or vacations—
can be carried over into other areas of family concern, using
the same balance of understanding that there are some decisions where there's full family input and some decisions that
are going to be made by the CEO.

It's also important to remember that those decisions
change. You don't have the same balance of authority in a
meeting with your sales reps that you do with your board of
directors, and you don't have the same balance in a discussion with your teenager that you do with your toddler.

And the reasons are pretty much the same. The sales
reps don't have the same awareness of the big picture that
the board of directors does, and your toddler doesn't have the
same awareness of the big picture that your teenager does.

When you're first teaching your children the jar system,
you'll spend a little time with them discussing their Quick
Cash Jar and what their limits are there. You might have
family rules about candy, or gum, or toy guns, or certain
kinds of comic books, but once your children know those
rules, there's not much to discuss. You'll probably spend a
good deal of time with them on their Medium-Term Savings
Jar, because they'll need to learn about how much things
cost and how long it will take to save up for them. You won't
talk to them at all about their Long-Term Savings Jar, because that's too far in the future for them to understand. For
now, they'll just be building up that savings habit.

You won't talk to your teenagers much about their
quick cash or their medium-term savings—they won't need
your help, and it'll basically be none of your business. But

you might well discuss their long-term savings—how much they have, how much they'll need for college, how much you'll be contributing, how they're going to get the rest.

By the same token, your preschooler or first grader doesn't need to understand the importance of getting into a good college in order for you to work on developing good study habits, any more than he has to understand the process of tooth decay in order for you to teach him the habit of brushing his teeth every day. But a sixteen-year-old has a much clearer idea of what college is and what his attitude is toward it. Much clearer, but not always as clear as he thinks it is.

Peg's discussions with Vincent about his grades were at an impasse, and Peg knew that she was dangerously close to falling into a mutual Gotcha! with him. But she wasn't going to leave it there. She was taking this stuff seriously; Gotcha! was no answer at work, and it wasn't going to be the answer at home, either.

"I don't need to do well in school, and I don't need to save for college, either," Vincent told her. "I'm not interested in being a lawyer, like you and Dad want me to be. I'm going to be an actor."

Peg knew that Vincent was too young to make a decision about what he was going to do for the rest of his life. But she knew, as well, that he wasn't too young to be starting to think about it in a way that deserved to be respected.

She was the household CEO. In this case, it didn't mean that she could give orders. It did mean that she was responsible for knowing enough to discuss the situation with Vincent.

"You're going to give me that speech about how not everyone makes it as an actor, aren't you?" Vincent asked. "You're not going to tell me you don't have faith in me, but that's what you'll be saying."

"No, I wasn't going to say that. So what kind of actor do you want to be? Like Keanu Reeves, maybe?"

"No," said Vincent. "I want to be a real actor. You know, like, with talent?"

"Yeah, I think I've heard of that," said Peg. "But then you know, not everyone in Hollywood has talent. Some of them just play the game. From what I know of you, you're something of a rebel. You don't put up with jerks or sell-outs. You might end up being a great actor, in experimental off-off-Broadway stuff. Then you'd be successful and respected, but you'd still need some extra money. And you'd really need an education then, because you'd have to use your wits to make a living. I was talking to my cousin Phil. He has a friend who's a terrific actor, and he does what he wants in the theater, which is work with kids and do children's theater, and he supports himself by running his own small ad agency. He writes and produces commercials, so he needs to know how to write and how to do the books for his own small business. He always knew he wanted to be an actor, but he always knew he'd have to study, because he didn't know what kind of actor he was going to be.

"You know what else he told me? The more you know, the better an actor you're going to be. An actor needs to have a very agile mind—even more than a lawyer, maybe. You never know what kind of part you're going to be called on to play, and you never know what kind of character you're going to need to understand. A lawyer needs to know certain things. An actor needs to know a little of everything."

"You're just trying to convince me to start getting good grades in school again, aren't you?" Vincent asked with a grin.

"And to keep saving for college," Peg said.

Peg knew that she hadn't settled the issue of Vincent's future with one conversation. But she didn't expect to. She knew that you take one battle at a time, and this one wasn't about making Vincent commit himself to college, it was about making sure Vincent didn't cut off college as an option, either in his grades or his long-term savings.

This was a first step, and a good one. Vincent continued contributing the full share of his income to his long-term savings. And, in fact, by the next semester he was back to applying himself at school and it was time to open up the subject of how much he would need for college and how he and the family were going to contribute to making up the rest.

Part III

Family-Friendly

The Other Side of the Equation

e've developed a curious relationship with the workplace. In a relatively short time we've gone from an era in which the usual—and expected—role for women was the housewife, to an era in which the working woman is the norm.

We've gone from the pink-collar ghetto to the glass ceiling.

And we've been the subject of a bewildering succession of myths, half-truths, and frequently half-baked theories. Some of these theories were okay; some of them bordered on the bizarre. But none of them answers the question of why people feel this obsessive need to theorize about the place of women in society, women in the home, women in the work-place. Do you see endless books and articles written about *men* in the workplace?

The truth is, everybody's got a theory, and theories are like Forrest Gump's mother's box of chocolates: we never know what we're going to get. The good news is, we don't have to swallow the stuff we don't like. If it's a yucky piece of chocolate, we can spit it out (into a tissue—manners are important). If it's a theory that makes sense to us, we can take it for what it's worth. And if it's one that seems to have absolutely no relationship at all to life as we understand it, we don't have to swallow the theory. We can say, "Thanks anyway, but that's not for me."

The bottom line is this: we all do the best we can. Sometimes we can figure out a little better way of getting what we want out of life, and sometimes advice, such as advice from a book, can actually help. I hope I've been able to help you with this book. Sometimes we can find a way to change the world so that it falls a little more in line with what we think is right, and I hope I'll be able to help you make a difference in that area, too.

We have a pretty good understanding of our own lives and how they work. If an expert tells us we're doing something all wrong, but it feels about right to us, then it's time to fall back on common sense—chances are we're doing all right and the expert is wrong. On the other hand, if we hear a new idea that rings a responsive chord, that fits in with what we already know and extends it a little, then it's something that's worth trying.

We women have been doing this all along. There was a time when the experts said we should all be like Donna Reed or Harriet Nelson or Carol Brady, and probably that was actually okay for some of us. But some of us had to work for a living, and we knew it. Some of us had drive and talent and ambition. We knew we could do a job as well as any man, and it felt right to be going out and doing it.

Then there came another group of experts who said that the only place for women was out in the workplace, competing with men on what had formerly been an all-male playing field. According to this group of experts, the whole idea that women were naturally maternal was a myth. It was a fairy tale dreamed up by men to keep women at home, barefoot and pregnant.

These were valuable and worthwhile theories for some of us, too, and they helped us give ourselves permission to get out and compete in the business world. The theorists of those days were a powerful and courageous group, and they really did liberate us from a stifling and repressive set of social rules. But that wasn't the whole story for all of us, either, and when some people began attaching a stigma to the woman who wanted to stay home and raise her children, we knew that this was a theory that didn't suit all of us.

And those were just the big theories. How about things like the women's dress-for-success theorists, who told us we all had to dress in dark suits and white blouses and little string ties?

When I started out in the executive training program at the Chase Manhattan Bank, a lot of people told me that I'd never be taken seriously in a man's world if I wore my nails long and put a colorful shade of nail polish on them. They told me that if I wanted to be professional, I'd have to get my hair cut short into a trim, businesslike "office cut."

Well, it just didn't feel right to me. I knew that it was important to look professional, but my instinct told me that there was more than one way to look professional. I was never going to look like a man, I didn't want to look like a man, and that wasn't going to be my model.

I'm still wearing long hair and long fingernails today, and if it ever looked out of place (I don't believe it ever did) it surely doesn't now.

Another observation that has gained a lot of currency in recent years, and that does have some relevance to some of our lives, is that many of us are spending more and more time at work, away from home.

This is certainly true, just on the basis of the almost complete integration of women into the workforce at most (not all) levels and over a tremendous range of businesses and industries. Seventy percent of all women, and over half of all mothers, work outside the home today.

What do these numbers mean? Well, they might mean something like this:

► The era of the two-income family is here to stay.
► The era of the single parent head of household is here to stay.
► Women have accepted the challenge of career and workplace, and they're not going to be denied—that's why a full 50 percent of women are still working outside the home even after they have children.
► Women are realizing the importance of those child-rearing years, and they are opting to stay home with their children whenever they can—that's why there's such a precipitous drop between the percentage of married women working and the total percent of working women.

Or how about all of the above? It all depends on who you are. If you're a single mom, like Alison, the theory that says two-income families are here to stay will give you a quick laugh, not much more.

Do the statistics prove that more women are choosing to work, or that more women are staying home to raise families?

"They don't prove a damn thing," says Peg. "I love my job. It drives me crazy sometimes, but what doesn't? I stayed home for three years with my first kid, a year and a half with my second. It put us into debt, but it was worth it—and we're digging our way out now, slowly but surely. So what category does that put me into—the 50 percent of moms who

work or the 50 percent of moms who stay home? You decide.
I'm too busy. I have better things to do with my time."

Most of us are too busy to spend a lot of time trying to
figure out which theory we fit into. One thing we can be sure
of, though: we're busy. There never seems to be enough time
in the day for everything.

Here's one theory about our time problem that might
have something to say to us, though. In the nineties, observers began to notice that people (men and women both,
but the observers were particularly pointing at women) were
spending more and more time at the office, less and less time
at home.

The observers were particularly pointing at women because for men this has always been true. For women, according to social theorists like Arlie Russell Hochschild in her
1997 book, *The Time Bind: When Work Becomes Home and*
Home Becomes Work, it became more and more true for the
nineties woman.

Hochschild's study found that most working parents, of
both sexes, are really drawn to their work. If their companies
have "family-friendly" policies, allowing for part-time work
or extended parental leave, they generally don't use them.

I spent a lot of time thinking about this one. Hochschild
and other authorities have pointed out that many women
and men consider the family-friendly policies that have
begun to enter workplaces in the nineties a major incentive
in choosing a job. Most people who work for family-friendly
companies, these studies found, pointed with pride to the enlightened attitudes of their employers. Often, they put those
family values high on their list of criteria for choosing an employer.

But they didn't take advantage of them all that often.
Why not?

Here's what I think. There are two powerful forces at

work here. First, there really are gratifications in the work-place that make it a desirable place to be. Some of those grat-ifications we found there, some of them we brought there. There's a sense of order, a sense of accomplishment, that we don't always find at home, although there are lessons there that we can take home. There is, perhaps most of all, a sense of completion—jobs there can actually be finished—that we don't always feel at home.

Second, "family-friendly" workplaces, for women, are still more than a little bit bogus. Attitudes in far too many workplaces are still stacked against us, and that's not okay, and it has to be changed.

Women still seem to be the exotic species, the one that doesn't quite fit in the workplace, or at least we (read this as we *men*) aren't quite sure how they fit in.

As a result, although there have been important ad-vances in this area, business as a whole hasn't quite moved beyond paying lip service to family friendliness in what are supposed to be our new family-friendly workplaces.

In the not-so-old days, the accepted wisdom was that it's a mistake to hire women for management jobs, executive jobs, jobs that require a lot of training, jobs that involve being promoted up the ladder, because they'll just get mar-ried and get pregnant and leave the workforce and . . . well, we can name that tune in two notes, can't we?

This accepted wisdom, by the way, might never have been true. According to an article by Sue Shellenbarger in the *Wall Street Journal* (December 20, 1995), the Bank of Montreal did a study on this very issue in 1991 and found that "being a woman does not mean reduced commitment."

The bank examined its personnel files over a period of several years and discovered that not only were female em-ployees *not* bailing out at a faster rate then men, they had longer service records than men at all levels except senior management. The only reason for the lower service records at that level was that there hadn't been any women at senior management levels until very recently. But the tale of the figures was clear. Women weren't quitting their jobs at any faster rate than men. They weren't leaving their careers because of childbirth.

The result of the Bank of Montreal survey was, I'm glad to say, a major new thrust toward promoting women. Between 1991 and 1995, the bank's percentage of female senior executives rose from 6 percent to 19 percent.

The stigma against any variation from the old-boy norm raised its anticipated head, with disgruntled men starting such rumors as "men are an endangered species around here." The company, to its credit, responded by opening personnel files to show that men were receiving their fair share of promotions.

However, that accepted wisdom has taken its toll on women over the years. We've had to prove that our family commitment would not stand in the way of our work commitment: the superwoman syndrome.

We got pretty good at it—so good that we made "superwoman" a part of the language. My first computer word-processing program, just a few years ago, had an automatic spellchecker that would stop cold at "superwoman" and inquire, snidely (well, I know that a dumb machine can't really be snide, but it always seemed snide to me): "Excuse me, but surely the word you're looking for is 'super*man*?'" The spellchecker in my current word-processing program, on the other hand, slides right over "superwoman," just as if it had known all along that it was a real word.

But why did we have to *be* superwomen? Because we had to prove that our careers came first, which meant we had to prove that our employers came first. Family? Did we have families? Our employers didn't want to know about it.

Naturally, that didn't mean that we thought about our families any less or that they became any less important to

us. It just meant that we didn't let anyone at the office know
about it.

We didn't talk about our kids—or if we did, we took our
cue from the men in the office as to what was acceptable and
what wasn't. A picture of the kids on the corner of the desk?
Certainly, that was okay—Mr. Bolton-Smythe, the vice president, had a picture of his kids, in a tasteful gold frame, on his
desk. And Mr. Bolton-Smythe could strut around the office
and announce proudly that young Bolton Bolton-Smythe had
been accepted at Dartmouth, just like his old man, harrumph, harrumph. So we could do that, too—without the
strutting. That would be unseemly in a woman. And we
could talk about touchdowns scored or home runs hit by
sons, although the rules for us were, once again, somewhat
different from the rules for Mr. Bolton-Smythe: it was best if
we sounded a little hesitant, suggesting that we didn't quite
know what a home run was but we knew it was a good thing.

That was pretty much the limit, according to the rules
that were unwritten and unstated, but clear enough nevertheless. We didn't talk about Gretchen's third grade report
card, on which the teacher had written that she showed unusual ability to work independently.

We certainly didn't talk about how we were taking
Steven in to be tested for reading problems, and we weren't
sure whether he needed glasses or whether he might be a little dyslexic; the last thing in the world we wanted to do was
give the impression that there might be problems at home
that would distract us from work.

But what about the bigger question: what was it, exactly, that we had to prove in the workplace?

Serious Like Who?

It seemed as though we were being called upon to prove that
we were serious, just like men. That our minds were on the

workplace, just like men. That we could keep from being distracted by frivolous, nonbusiness concerns, just like men. That we could be mature and dependable and focused, just like men.

Excuse me. But I went to work in the banking industry in 1972, and I worked alongside men for twenty years (almost nothing but men, when I started), and while I worked alongside men who were mature and dependable and reasonably work-focused, they wouldn't necessarily have been my only role models for those qualities.

They didn't meet the superemployee standards that were set for us. While we were constantly under the gun to prove ourselves—which meant assiduously taking all that time that we might have frittered away talking about toilet training, doll tea parties, Easy Bake ovens, and sweet sixteens, and instead spending that time learning more about the business—they were talking about sports, and lawn tractors, and other perfectly normal interests that anyone should have a right to talk about.

The point here is that whatever you were told to the contrary, it *is* possible to have a career and a life at the same time—just like men. But we're a little afraid to do that, and not without reason. We grew used to a double standard, where the things men discussed casually were accepted as a normal part of the workday because they were familiar, and the things women discussed casually were seen as distractions because they were unfamiliar.

So here's the truth about why we don't take advantage of family-friendly policies: we don't entirely trust them yet. And we're probably right not to.

Project Manager: Daisy Jaffe, thirty-seven, attorney. Married, mom of Hettie, seven; and Zach, three.

Ever since I've had my children I've made absolutely no secret about how important my kids are in my life and that if I have to reschedule something because of an important family thing, I'll do it. But I had established a pretty strong reputation in my field before I had children, so that made a difference. I have a friend in the office where I work, and she had twins last year. They were adorable.

She came back to work after about two months of maternity leave (the firm allows more, but that was all she took) and when I stopped by her office, maybe a week later, I noticed that she had no pictures of the twins anywhere. I asked her why not, and she said, "I don't think that's the kind of statement I want to make."

Statement! I couldn't imagine feeling like that. I don't just have pictures of my kids in my office, I have refrigerator art. I bring in pictures my kids draw and hang them all over my office. So I guess I'm making a statement, but it's a statement about who I really am, not who I want people in the office to think I am.

I can understand how she feels, though. If I were really hell-bent on making partner in the firm, I can't say for sure that I wouldn't be doing the same thing that she's doing, although I hope I wouldn't.

The truth is, when I had Hettie, I did make child-over-career decisions. I'd been the hottest young lawyer in my field; I'd billed more hours than any other associate in the state. But I took one look at her and decided I didn't have to hold on to that title. I took the mommy track. I worked out an arrangement with my firm that gave me a lot more flexibility to be with Hettie, and then with Hettie and Zach.

But I made partner anyway. It took a few more years, but I did it.

What would be my advice to women in the office? Be yourself. If it feels right to put up refrigerator art all over your office, go ahead and do it—unless you're working in a place that has a rule of no art at all. But don't do it just to make a statement, any more than you should keep pictures of your kids out of your office because you're afraid of making a statement.

This is an issue that's still in a period of transition, and it's not moving along anywhere near as quickly as the business and corporate world likes to say it is.

Nobody is addressing the real issue, and here's what it is. We still go to work in a society that considers certain company-sponsored activities, or company-underwritten activities, to be a part of the mainstream culture of the workplace, yet still considers others to be special accommodations, with all the dubious distinction that confers.

That's why women like Daisy have to make "mommy track" choices that *should not have to be made.*

And that's why we keep having to manage projects that should not have to be managed, like the one my friend Sarah describes.

Project Manager: Sarah Miller, forty-four, systems analyst. Divorced, mom of Steven, fourteen; and Jane, eleven.

My biggest project, it seems, was my mother, who kept telling me, when I started my career, "Someday you're going to have to choose between your career and your children."

When I had Steven, virtually her first words were, "Now you're going to have to choose."

I continued with my career. By her lights, I didn't make the right choice. By my estimation, there was no choice to make. It took more work than it ought to have to arrange a life around both family and career, but it wasn't impossible. Much to her chagrin, I might add.

However, she has managed, ever since, to keep the issue alive. Every time one of my kids screws up—and it doesn't happen very often, I might add; my kids are exceptionally good kids, and I'm so proud of them—she'll say with a deep sigh, "Well, *you* made your choice." A C-minus on a report card, a failure to write her a prompt thank-you note: "Well, you *made* your choice."

When Jim and I got divorced, she said, "Well, of course you did. I could have predicted it. You earn more money than he does." Jim and I had our problems, Lord knows, but that wasn't one of them. Jim was actually always supportive of my work, and since it's turned out to be a reasonably amicable divorce, he still is.

Yes, you're still swimming against the stream as a working

mom. No matter how much things have changed, they haven't changed all that much.

The project with my mother is to keep reminding myself that she represents one reality, but it doesn't have to be the only one.

Changing the Norm

The workplace culture can justify taking an afternoon off from work to play golf, but it can't justify taking the afternoon off to go to a child's dance recital. To test that theory out, try hitting the links any weekday between nine and five. No one there but retirees? Not on your life. That country club, even that public golf course, will be chock-full of foursomes made up of corporate executives, middle managers, lawyers, financial planners, and sales reps.

Now stop at a dance recital for eight- to ten-year-olds. How many corporate types will you see there? It won't be an impressive number.

Ah, you'll hear, you don't understand. You can get work done out on the golf course. It's a great place to clear your mind and get down to some real business talk. In fact, there's even a course offered on how to use golf as a business conferencing tool.

Just try this as an experiment sometime: ask the vice president in charge of marketing what the quarterly sales figures are while he's in the middle of his backswing.

People who play golf take it seriously, even if they say they don't. No one goes out onto the golf course to let golf take a backseat to business.

When you think about it, a Little League game would be a much better place to get some business done. Little boys in baseball uniforms are adorable, but they aren't totally absorbing except for the few minutes when your own son is up at bat. Their games would actually make a terrific backdrop for a business discussion: just enough of a distraction to give inspiration a chance to burst in, but not so totally distracting that they'd absolutely cut you off from working, as long as you did it quietly and politely from up in the bleachers.

Of course, no one would actually do this. It makes far too much sense.

Look at it this way: Suppose a great golf pro like Tiger Woods comes to town, and by some miracle he offers to give some pointers to anyone in your office who wants them. It would take about ten seconds for the average boss to decide that, as a matter of fact, the office can really afford to be closed down for one day; we can always make up the work, after all.

No pretense of getting some work done out on the golf course, or the other popular excuse about making some great contacts. No, this one would be marked down as a morale booster, something to bring the whole office staff together.

There's nothing wrong with that. Morale boosters are wonderful things for a company.

All right, now suppose that, instead of Tiger Woods, it's a great child development expert like T. Berry Brazelton who comes to town and offers to give parenting tips to anyone in your office who wants them. Does the whole office get the day off this time?

You know the answer.

The myth is that men are the serious workers and women are still dilettantes. But that's nowhere close to reality. And it is not okay to let this last great male myth of the workplace go unchallenged.

It's an insidious myth, and a pervasive one. It's the reason why "family-friendly" is an idea whose time hasn't quite come yet. It's the reason, in fact, why "family-friendly" is a term that has to be used at all. The minute you coin a phrase like "family-friendly workplace," you're ghettoizing the concept. You're making it sound like a special concession that the company is making, and as soon as you make something sound like a special concession, you're making it sound like something that is not quite deserved.

Have you ever heard of a golf-friendly workplace?

Integrating Family and Home

In the first societies, there was no separation at all between work and home. People lived together in clans—they hunted together, they foraged together—from the very young to the very old.

That remained true for thousands of years. It was true in feudal societies, it was true in agrarian societies, it was true in the communities of pre-industrial society. It was true in the American heartland Little House stories of Laura Ingalls Wilder. Laura's family didn't stop being a family, and working together as a family, when they moved from the little house on the prairie to the little town on the prairie. They had delineated social roles, and there was certainly gender separation (though not absolute gender separation) in those roles, but family and work were still an integrated whole.

That didn't change until the Industrial Revolution. Machines revolutionized the way work was done, and the workplace had to accommodate to machines, which meant that people also had to accommodate. Whether they were men, in the mills and auto plants, or women, at the sewing machines in the sweatshops of the garment industry, they had to become synchronous with the machines.

The people who went out to work—and they were mostly men or young women who hadn't started families yet—separated themselves from the world of family. The world of home and children became a kind of secret world that men didn't know about, just as the world of work and machines became a secret world that women didn't know about.

It was during this era that the sentimental Victorian stereotype of family life was developed. It was during this era that phrases like "sainted motherhood" came into being, and it was then that Mother's Day was invented. This concept of the workplace as a machine began to change, ever so slowly at first, in the second quarter of the twentieth century. Social and economic theorists began to point out flaws in the philosophy of efficiency through making workers subordinate to machinery.

In our era, the changes in the workplace became sea changes. They became a movement. The office, even the factory, was now seen as organic, not mechanical. The people instead of the machines became the center.

The workplace became more like a family. But it was an odd kind of family. It was built around men's awareness, men's sensibilities, and most of all, men's separation from home and the family that was there. The name for work units in the office has always been "team," which is a masculine concept (think of sports teams and military units).

When women came into the workplace, we brought innovations in problem solving and more humanizing elements. But the one taboo that we have not been able to confront head-on is the taboo that says work is work and home is home, and never the twain shall meet.

Family, Inc.

Those of us who are working at the office—and running our families at home at the same time—need to remember that the marketplace really isn't sufficiently family-friendly yet and that this is not satisfactory.

This is the other side of Mom, Inc. Let's call it Family, Inc. We have to keep on confronting the received wisdom that says some kinds of integration of life and work are more acceptable than other kinds.

We have to get back to the basic social and organizational structure of human society, which is that we're all workers and we're all family members. That's the way we were designed, and separation between these two roles is unnatural.

Right now, we can go into interviews for new jobs, or we can talk to our bosses about restructuring our present jobs, and we can ask for, and reasonably expect to get:

▶ Flex time
▶ Job sharing
▶ Liberal maternity/paternity leave
▶ Telecommuting (for some jobs)

Here are benefits that some companies are giving right now:

▶ In-house day care centers
▶ Company-subsidized day care centers
▶ Sick leave for a child's illness

But what about:

▶ An ongoing arrangement with a temp agency to provide temporary nannies to stay at home with the kids for a few days, a week, a month?
▶ An ongoing arrangement with a visiting nurse service to provide short-term care for a sick child at home, even on short notice (it's 6:45 A.M., little Bobby's tummy hurts, and you have an important sales conference at 10 A.M.)?
▶ A special arrangement to provide nannies for employees who have to travel on company business?
▶ A corporation-sponsored summer camp?
▶ A supervised on-the-job playroom so that parents of preschoolers (of either sex) who suddenly and unexpectedly find themselves taking care of the kids for the afternoon can still go to work?
▶ A playroom that's close enough to the work area so that parents can take coffee breaks with their preschool kids?
▶ Corporate accounts with restaurants or amusement parks for family birthday or holiday parties?

Do these requests give the impression that women are suddenly demanding that the world be handed to them on a silver platter?

If not, then why aren't we asking for them? Many corporations, during the boom years of the nineties, have become increasingly open to a wide range of negotiated perks. They haven't, for the most part, been this particular set of perks, but they should be.

If these demands sound like too much to ask, then it's really time to ask ourselves: *Why?*

I don't think any one of these demands is remotely unreasonable. I don't think that all of them together, as a package, are remotely unreasonable.

I think that we have a right to ask—I think it's normal and healthy to ask—that men and women return to the basis upon which society was structured: the synchronicity of work and family.

These are, essentially, no different from the perks that businesses give employees all the time.

Look at how things are. If a secretary quits suddenly or develops an illness that will require him to miss a week of work, what company is going to tell a busy executive, "Sorry, but you're going to have to do all your own filing for the next couple of weeks. You're going to have to do all your own copying and faxing, schedule your own appointments, and remember when and where they are. You'll have to take all your own calls, place all your own calls, and wait on hold for as long as it takes the other party to pick up. You'll have to type all your own letters. And if you don't know where all the office supplies are kept . . . better learn."

No company is going to do that, because no company wants its busy executives distracted by doing all those things. They aren't the most productive use of an executive's time. If the secretary calls in at 9 A.M. to say he just eloped to

Hawaii and won't be in, there's a structure in place to make sure that an experienced temp arrives in a timely fashion.

How is this different from having a structure in place to ensure that a nanny is available at equally short notice?

Many corporations, in these enlightened days, will provide rehabilitation for an executive who's developed a drinking problem or a drug problem. There'll be time off; there'll be counseling. The company will pay the expenses of a stay in a private rehab clinic. This happens a lot in major corporations—and almost always to men.

Why is this a more acceptable corporate expense than a visiting nurse service for sick kids?

And, for that matter, why are women asked (directly or implicitly) in job interviews, "How do we know you won't need time off to have a baby?" when men aren't asked "How do we know you won't need time off for alcoholism or drug addiction rehab?"

What about this one? How is expecting a corporation to have corporate accounts with a playland for a family birthday party different from the same corporation's picking up the tab for an employee's country club membership? (Well, one difference is that the playland would be a lot cheaper.)

Why is it okay to take a couple of hours off in the middle of the day to work out at a health club but not to chaperone your first grader's field trip to a cider mill?

Loyalty and the Office

Recently, a headhunter called me regarding someone who had given my name as a reference. We talked for a few minutes, and I asked her what she considered the greatest problem confronting American businesses today. She didn't hesitate.

"Loyalty," she said. "No one stays with one company

anymore. People are constantly jumping—two years and out. I can tell you, I have no complaints. Business is booming for me."

Two years and out. In 1972, when I began my career in banking, it cost $250,000 for a company to train a skilled, high-level employee. That figure, I knew, included the time, facilities, and staff needed for the training, and the salary and perks of the new employee during the approximately two years it takes before a new person knows enough to make a positive contribution to the company. Now, two years and the employee is gone, just as she's in a position to make a significant contribution. It's a buyer's market for skilled and experienced people.

The headhunter and I talked a little more. "What's the biggest problem that you deal with as a member of the workforce?" I asked.

Again, she didn't have to think twice.

"Child care," she said.

"What if you had the opportunity to work for a company that provided temp nannies and temp home nursing services for your kids?" I asked.

"I'd go to work for them in a second," she said. "Those things would be very nearly more important than the job description."

"Suppose a company offered a free college education for your kids if you stayed with them more than five years? Or a sabbatical after fifteen years, so that you and your family could spend three months on an educational or spiritual self-improvement property at the company's expense?"

"There aren't any companies like that," she said.

In fact, there are, although they're still a small minority. I happened to have talked to one that morning. Nuveen, a financial services company in Chicago, has all those services. Nuveen spokesperson Kathy Flanagan, who explained them to me, began by saying: "Companies today have to be cre-

ative to help address life-balance issues with employees.
Having experienced these tensions firsthand in my own career, and watching the same issues emerge a generation later
for my daughters, I know that these kinds of corporate
changes make a difference in the effectiveness of a company
by increasing a sense of community, fostering greater efficiency and loyalty of employees. and retaining high-caliber
individuals."

Nuveen's scholarship plan guarantees, to employees
who've been with the company at least five years, at least a
one-year college scholarship for each of their children, with
the possibility of continued scholarships for good academic
standing.

Fifteen-year employees can receive a six-week paid sabbatical at full pay and with full participation in all benefit
plans, to be spent on "travel, education, community involvement, or any other outside interest."

"If there were more companies like that, there'd be a lot
less demand for people like me," the headhunter said.

"How about a company that you could call in and say,
'We'll have to reschedule tomorrow's meeting, because I
have to go to my daughter's dance recital'?" I asked.

"Now you are kidding," she said.

"Now I am kidding," I admitted. "But do you place people with companies where you can call in and say, 'We'll
have to reschedule tomorrow's meeting, because I have an
important golf date?' "

"Oh, golf!" she said. "That's different, isn't it? Sure,
most of the companies I deal with will let you do that. But I
suppose we have to look on the bright side. It gives us
women a lot of quiet time in the office to get work done."

I don't mean to keep harping on golf, but there's a guy
in New Jersey who has an excellent business doing golf seminars for major corporations. His promotional material em-
phasizes the importance of being at your best for a "six-hour

sales call on the golf course" and offers executives "greater confidence in their golf game and in their relationship-building efforts with their clients . . . one of the key benefits of the program is that corporations can now see a better return on investment for their customer entertainment dollar."

Just to make sure we have this straight . . . this is a return on investment on *golf* that we're talking about here. What we're talking about is paying an employee of a company to go out *all day* and play golf. And further, we're talking about paying an outside consultant to come in, on company time, and teach that company's employees to do it.

Return on Investment

If companies can justify golf seminars on the basis of a projected return on investment, they certainly should be able to justify providing you with a temp nanny in terms of return on investment. Most companies can't provide you with a temp nanny for only one reason: because they've never done it. It hasn't been identified as a priority, and therefore no mechanism has been put in place.

Not every woman in the workforce will have the clout to demand these changes. Someone looking for a job as a middle-level supervisor, or a copy editor, couldn't open up negotiations by saying "I'll take the job if you'll provide a temp nanny service." But highly skilled people, in fields for which there's a high demand, could start asking for this as a perk. People in fields that have strong unions, like teachers, could ask for it as a benefit. There's no reason why men, as well as women, shouldn't want this, too, and shouldn't include it as a demand. And if it starts happening—if we create Family, Inc.—then we all benefit from it. Men as well as women.

Both *Working Mother* and *Working Woman* magazines publish an annual list of the most family-friendly companies, with comments on each one. There's also a website, www.workfamily.com, which gathers and posts articles and government documents that spotlight other companies with enlightened policies.

These family-friendly policies, as they develop, will give those of us who work outside the home a better chance to create a work/home balance. And however we structure our time, that balance in our lives and in our skills is what we're looking for.

Epilogue

Mom, Inc.

All of these workplace reforms should be implemented, and most of them are being introduced by at least a few companies. The movement is still slow, but it's going in the right direction. Catalyst, Inc., a nonprofit research and advisory organization working with business to advance women, has reported that work/family balance has become an employer's issue in the nineties as more and more employers discover how much it affects recruitment, productivity, and employee loyalty.

This is good news. But equally important, the fact that the workplace is moving in our direction proves that we're right. Our instincts are good ones; our values are solid.

We can see that being proved out in the workplace. It's been a tough fight, and there's more tough fighting ahead. But when we can see real change, and real successes, it gives us heart.

These changes are projects. Getting parental leave or

backup child care—these are things that can be visualized, worked for, and achieved. And once they are achieved, we know it. We can take credit for them, and gain confidence to go on.

And that's why it's so important that we bring all of this home.

We need to bring our confidence home. We *can* make a difference. We know this, of course—as mothers, we make the greatest difference in our children's lives. But sometimes we only know it in general. Our workplace experience tells us that we can make specific and definite changes. We can see problems and solutions. We can set goals and attain them.

And that's what we need to remember at home, too. We don't have to fall into the same routine, day after day. We don't have to do things because someone else, or everyone else, says they've always been done that way.

We don't have to assume that things can't be changed, because we know that they can be.

We don't have to accept that things are out of our control, because we know they don't have to be.

As the CEO of Mom, Inc., you're in charge of the most dynamic company the world has ever known. It's the most challenging and it's the most stimulating. It produces the most important products. It works because you make it work with all that talent and drive and managerial skill, all that vision, all those personnel skills that you've already proved you have.

Index